BEAT THE PRICE OBJECTION
Building Confidence in Your Telling Price

RICK DAVIS

Hard Knock Press

Copyright © 2021 by Rick Davis. All rights reserved.

No part of this book may be used or reproduced in any manner whatsoever without written permission except in the case of brief quotations embodied in critical articles and review. For information, address rickdavis@buildingleaders.com.

To book Rick as a speaker for your next event or to learn more about sales and sales management training programs for your company, visit **www.buildingleaders.com**.

First published by Hard Knock Press, September 2021

Cover design by Lynda Van Duerm
Interior layout by Vickie Swisher, Studio 20|20

ISBN: 978-0-9847114-6-8 (hc)
ISBN: 978-0-9847114-5-1 (pb)

Library of Congress Control Number: 2021917872

BEAT THE PRICE OBJECTION
Building Confidence in Your Telling Price

*For the women.
It has always been the women who
provide me the strength to forge onward.
They are warriors and warrior-leaders.*

Contents

Acknowledgements ix
Foreword xi
Preface – The Price Objection xv

1	It's a Telling Price 1
2	It's a Million Points 9
3	Dirty Water at the Mouth of the River 21
4	Established Pricing 33
5	Speed is the Enemy of Profit 49
6	You Choose Your Customers 61
7	Abundance Happens Between Your Ears 71
8	People Care How Much You Care 83
9	You Can't Measure What You Can't See 95
10	Stop Bidding and Start Proposing 103
11	The Heat of Battle is Too Late 119
12	Career Security 131

Epilogue: Going Through the Motions 141
About the Author 146

Acknowledgements

Well…I wrote the book! I only mention it because a lot of people tell me they would like to write a book. They say they want to be authors, but probably don't want to write a book. It's a huge undertaking to write, re-write, edit, and delete massive sections of words you take very personally. Thus, I hope you acknowledge that anyone who actually completes the task deserves some bit of acknowledgement. And others too! Especially…

Meg Naulty is my wife who endures all the ups, downs, and sideways a writer goes through to finish a manuscript and bring words to life. Thank you for it all. I love you with all my heart.

Ellice Herman is my teammate who manages an online learning platform, promotes our business relentlessly, organizes and manages events, and to top it off, is one hell of an editor. She catches the mistakes, although if you find any, it's my fault and not hers. She provides amazing insights into content. She patiently reads and re-reads every sentence, sometimes alone and often with me. To you, Ellice, I say thank you for it all.

A few years ago, my friend and mentor, Bill Lee, was my partner in delivering lectures throughout the United States to help salespeople cope with the ubiquitous price objection. We spent time golfing, getting to know each other, and mostly just trying to help people deal with the most fundamental problem for our profession. He also was gracious enough to craft a foreword for this book. Thank you, Bill.

Rick Schumacher is the publisher and editor for the *LBM Journal*. He is a tireless entrepreneur who always seems to find time that allows me to bounce an idea off him or gain his valuable advice. He was the first person to read my first of a half dozen "final drafts" and instantly gave me the encouragement to get to the finish line.

Vickie Swisher is the layout designer of my last two books and will be as long as I have the privilege of working with her. It is one thing to see a book in raw manuscript and an entirely different thing to have an artist bring it to life. She does so beautifully with grace in spite of the ridiculous deadlines I foist upon her.

Lynda Van Duerm, as always, thank you for your wonderful design skills. I feel privileged to know you. Lynda has been designing my ads, brochures, and book covers from the very start. She is amazing.

I thank Louis Segovia. He's a salesman, but also a great resource for me to rely and the man who has helped me produce a successful book publishing company as a little side hustle to my everyday work.

Never will I write a book without acknowledging some extremely important people in my life, specifically Bob Eckert, Mark Hansen, Tom Latourette, and Kathy Ziprik, all of whom helped me launch. I also feel remiss if I don't mention my sister-in-law, Beth Naulty, who manages to provide amazing support and allows me to read extended passages to her for review.

Lastly, I acknowledge you! If you've come this far, keep going. Read the book! I guarantee it will produce amazing return on your investment in time.

Foreword

I can tell you that there's no obstacle that salespeople struggle with more prevalent than the price objection. It is the first obstacle every salesperson must learn to deal with, and few salespeople ever successfully master the art of getting what Rick calls in this book, the "Telling Price."

Most buyers will test salespeople, especially new salespeople. With years of experience and well-practiced negotiation tactics, buyers can be brutal, especially with salespeople who are unschooled at defending their prices. Buyers use tactics such as, "You can do better than that" or "Here's what I am authorized to pay, take it or leave it."

Many years ago, I watched one of my mentors hear a buyer use a clever tactic by saying, "I'll tell you what I want you to do, I want you to look me right in the eye and tell me that you're not selling any of your customers at a lower price than you are offering me." It was a completely unexpected statement and, because it would have been a lie to say otherwise, it worked! Since then, I have learned and shared with many salespeople techniques to overcome the price objection in its many forms.

To sell at your *telling price*, you must have confidence in yourself and your company. Salespeople who fall into the trap of letting buyers intimidate them into quoting a price prematurely will rarely achieve their gross margin goals. And a salesperson who routinely caves in and reduces the initial price offering will rarely if ever know the joy of selling at their target price.

I became a Rick Davis fan when I began reading his columns in the construction supply industry trade press. At the time I was writing a column for a competitive publication, so I always read with interest Rick's articles on sales and especially enjoyed his writing style and his insights into the profession we share.

My respect for Rick grew with each passing year. He was the kind of person I wanted to know better, so since my son lived in a Northwestern suburb of Chicago, Rick and I decided to meet for lunch. What was supposed to be a short meeting before lunch turned into a full day of getting to know each other.

Both Rick and I had enough respect for each other to begin discussing how we might turn our new friendship into a business venture, so we pulled out our calendars and carved out several weeks to conduct a series of sales seminars throughout the United States, specifically to help salespeople overcome the price objection. The venture was highly successful and the next year we decided to do it again, selecting some cities that we were not able to schedule the year before.

Rick's speaking style has its roots in his intimate knowledge of the selling profession, but also from the education he received at the University of Michigan in Ann Arbor. Educationally speaking, Rick is an economist. He doesn't just understand sales, he understands business and the role sales plays in a successful business. He develops theoretical models, like the one in this book, that have been tested in reality and work.

I found Rick to be a highly structured individual. He is not someone who "wings" it. He is disciplined, organized, and approaches his profession similarly. When he makes a sales call, writes a book, takes his bicycle on a 50-mile ride, or delivers a keynote address, he does so in a highly structured manner. You cannot possibly spend much time around Rick and not respect the man's discipline and the degree to which he does his homework.

Few professional speakers have received the awards Rick has received as a member of the National Speakers Association, a worldwide organization. He is one of only a handful of professional speakers who have earned the Certified Speaking Professional (CSP) designation, the NSA's only earned award.

Rick has spent his entire career dealing with the price objection. He knows firsthand the stress salespeople go through when their prices are challenged. When you finish reading this book, you will understand negotiating skills 101, the basics of dealing with the price objection by never giving up anything without at least attempting to get something in return. You will learn the fundamentals of pricing profitably. Ultimately, you will understand why Rick says, "Success happens when you stick to a game plan."

Bill Lee
Lee Resources, Inc.

Preface – The Price Objection

I believe the price objection is like dirty water at the mouth of the river. You can try cleaning all the river pollution at the mouth, but the garbage keeps flowing. You must address the problems upstream. The price objection works the same way. If you want to get your price, you must address issues early in the selling process.

The thesis of my book came from unexpected inspiration. I was riding my bicycle during a beautiful summer day in southwestern Michigan. I passed in front of a lovely country home where an SUV sat in the yard with a sign that read "$2,600 O.B.O." The O.B.O. stands for "or best offer," or at least I think it does. I'd prefer it stood for "or better offer," but don't imagine a lot of buyers would offer more than $2,600.

This price in the windshield, of course, represented an *asking price*. The seller signaled they were very willing to negotiate, and essentially invited it. They conceded the price was only a guideline and thus dirtied the water upstream long before a negotiation was instigated. I thought further about the nature of selling a used car versus a new one. If you really think about it, the used car presents a distinct sales advantage. An identical version of a new car can be bought in a lot of places, but a used car has its own unique story. That seller should have felt confident in the price of that car because it was a one-of-a-kind offer.

You are also a one-of-a-kind offer. You deserve your price even if the products you sell are similar to others. The products might be alike, but sales performances and support differ. I was once told that getting your price is a matter of self-esteem, and I agree. The purpose of my book is to get your agreement too!

It's easy to presume you are victimized by a tough market or aggressive negotiators. And certainly, in many cases, this is true. That being said, in dozens of subtle ways, salespeople are their own worst enemies. They diminish their value by inviting price negotiations. Without using the phrasing "or best offer," salespeople signal there is wiggle room in the price with body language and verbal invitations to negotiation such as asking "how the price came in" or the opportunity for the "last look" at pricing before a decision is made. I could write more…but you get the idea. In some form or another, however unintentionally, salespeople indicate that a negotiation is to be had.

The asking price becomes a starting point rather than the final price, which makes the job for professional buyers easy and encourages them to routinely "test the water." It's a good tactic because it so often works. My favorite sentence in the book states that testing the waters for a better price "works often enough that this negotiation tactic of professional buyers becomes ritualized and supported by our own fears."

We should be delivering telling prices, not asking prices, the concept which inspired this book. The sales journey to higher profits is told here by letting you see inside the mind of a salesperson, Noah, as he confronts a typical price objection. The journey illustrates that the price objection is not solved during a last-minute negotiation. Profitable transactions and relationships are the sum total of exchanges occurring long before a price is delivered.

There are no guarantees and I do not exist in a fantasyland. I understand there are times to negotiate and even sacrifice a little to get the sale, but you will discover when and how to do that properly by absorbing the lessons in this book. The real discovery is how to limit the degree of negotiations you face; cope effectively with countertactics; and most importantly find the right buyers who ultimately won't even raise the price objection. It's not an asking price; it's a telling price. Ultimately, this book will teach you how to believe it and earn it.

1

It's a Telling Price

"Your price is too high. You'll have to come down a little bit."

I have heard these words many times during my sales career. John Henderson is saying them to me right now. Every time this occurs, I expect I'll remain stoic in the face of the challenge we salespeople call *the price objection*, but I am not calm.

I am beyond not calm. My palms are sweaty. I can feel my heart throbbing. Even with all the training and preparation for this moment, I'm nervous. If you have ever sold anything, you probably know the feeling of anxiety when a buyer says your price is too high. It's a pressure moment we all face.

My name is Noah. I am a salesman.

2   BEAT THE PRICE OBJECTION

His name is John Henderson. He is the owner of Mahogany Builders.

John is a prospective new customer who could be worth lots of business for years to come. His firm handshake and lack of callouses prove he has not spent any recent time wielding a hammer or laboring on a jobsite. He is an imposing 6'5" that towers over me even when we are sitting at his desk. His shelves are stocked with business books, industry awards, and numerous event photos of his family which look more like poached pictures of magazine models. His pastel green golf shirt and groomed, salt and pepper hair amplify the tan he has earned while golfing and boating, hobbies typically reserved for the affluent. In short, he exudes power and success. I am intimidated.

He runs his business from the guest house behind a sprawling 6,200 square foot Tudor mansion in Lake Forest, Illinois. Mahogany Builders is a premier developer of custom homes on the exclusive Lake Michigan shore north of the Chicago suburbs. He is known to be a challenging negotiator, but a very loyal customer once you earn his business. Currently, he is staring at me with a dubious look that indicates my price is altogether unreasonable.

He didn't even read the proposal. Instead, John has turned quickly to the last page and paused while looking at the price. Now he is looking me in the eye and giving the bad news. He isn't considering the contributions I will, and already have provided his company, which were described in the proposal. He is ignoring all the work that my coworkers could do for him. He is saying that my company, my products, and I amount to nothing more than a number.

He is putting me to the test by asking for a "little" more. A set of stapled papers, my proposal, is flipped open to the last page and resting on John's desk. He remains silent and stares while waiting for a concession. He isn't making a counteroffer. He is brusquely stating I am too high on the price. End of story.

I'm processing. One little signature stands between me and a lucrative contract. It's my turn to respond and a younger, inexperienced version of me would cave immediately. The problem is that I am now experienced enough, or should be, to fend off the anxiety of the moment. The split-second hesitation feels like an eternity.

The difference for me today and all the other times I've encountered the price objection is that you're in my head seeing the synapses of my brain firing on all cylinders. I'm overly amped up about the opportunity. If I get this sale, my new client could purchase a few hundred thousand dollars of material, just in the coming year. Over the life of the relationship, millions of sales dollars hang in the balance, not to mention a tidy boost to my income. He would instantly become one of my largest accounts.

It is easy to rationalize a lower price. I'm going to get paid well on this account even if I give a few dollars to make the sale. My commission will be reduced a little, but a little commission on a big sale is better than no commission on a lost one.

The price objection once again is exposing the secret doubt in my abilities. My very good sales results in recent months mean nothing in the heat of this current negotiation battle. I am nervous and fearful of losing a great opportunity. I'm sure I am not alone. Even highly experienced veterans get anxious during negotiations.

My mentor, Abe Isaacson, told me that the doubts are good because it means I am thinking about the job critically. Abe hired me a few months back from a competitor. He is over 60 years old but has an enthusiasm that makes him seem younger. He's a fit cyclist with thinning grey hair. He manages to look incredibly professional at all times without overdressing. "Get your business clothing professionally laundered. That's the secret," he told me with a wink when I asked how a salesperson should dress. Abe is clearly admired by the other salespeople for reasons that become apparent as I get to know him.

As I sit here with John, facing the pressure of another price objection in a long series of them during my career, Abe's voice rings in my ears. "Selling is a process," he often says," but unlike any other business discipline. Accountants deal with numbers. Managers deal with inventory. The input of numbers and inventory create highly predictable outcomes. Salespeople deal with unpredictability. The input of sales performance produces uncertain outcomes. Salespeople deal with buyers who are temperamental, opinionated, and occasionally combative. Buyers negotiate. Numbers and inventory don't have opinions and they don't talk back."

I always got a chuckle out of that last statement. It was Abe's way of illustrating that selling is a game with uncertain outcomes. "You make moves in games that don't always work," Abe says. "In sales, you try your best, hope to do everything right and, yet still lose a sale." Abe raises a finger and widens his eyes as his best impersonation of a mad scientist. "However!" he adds, "There is usually a *'best move'* in each selling situation, even if the outcome is not guaranteed."

John Henderson's price objection is one of those moments

where there are better moves than the one I instinctively want to make, which is to figure what price he wants to pay. My mind is cluttered. It is hard to not be emotional when the stakes are high. I am thinking about getting the sale and celebrating my success. The voices of reason are trying to overcome conflicting emotions between the fear of a lost sale and excitement for a new one.

The words of Abe Isaacson ring in my ear. He frequently says, "You will never know the joy, power, and satisfaction of holding your price and winning a sale until you've held your price and lost one."

"It's not an opinion," Abe says about this last statement. "It's a law. At some point, the salesperson *must* hold firm. If the salesperson's first reaction in the face of a combative negotiation is always to relent, then the salesperson will never know if they can get their price. Sooner or later, a salesperson needs to hold the price and risk a sale. The logic is irrefutable. If you don't hold your price at some point, you prove you are *always* willing to negotiate."

"Yeah, right," I am silently saying to Abe right now. "Except that we're talking about a huge opportunity here. I know you've taught me to hold my price and there are times I have. But this is a big-league sale. This situation is different." I realize my retort is what all salespeople say. The other thing they say is the very thing I am thinking right now, which is, "I'll try on a future, less important sale."

My instinct is luring me to ask John where the price needs to be. It's the worst move in the negotiation game because it essentially tells the buyer to determine the price and, worse yet, indicates you have no clue where your price ought to be. Furthermore, it gives the buyer negotiation leverage by dropping the "negotiation anchor." That's what Abe calls the counteroffer. It's a baseline price that might not be expected by the buyer but establishes psychologically a negotiation foundation.

"The anchor sets up the 'split,'" Abe would say. "It's a negotiation tactic they are taught as purchasing professionals. They are 'testing the waters' to see if there is room to move. The problem is that they presume our price is an anchor too, merely a starting point. It's not. It's an expected price for our value, or at least it should be. It's not an asking price.

"It's a *telling* price. We're telling the buyer how much the goods will cost, but the common practice of buyers is to seek any available discount. It works often enough that this negotiation tactic of professional buyers becomes ritualized and supported by our own fears."

I quickly dismiss the idea of dropping my price and consider asking for an apples-to-apples comparison, which means verifying that my competitor (presuming there is one) is bidding the identical list of material. However, I remember Abe saying, "the apples-to-apples *move* is a decent tactic because it ensures you're on a level playing field but can be received by the buyer as a tacit agreement that the lowest price *should* win. If you have confidence that you've handled the details properly, you shouldn't have to invest time reviewing the work of a competitor. At best, apples-to-apples price comparisons delay negotiations unnecessarily and, at worst, lead to price wars."

Abe talks about the *right move for each situation* and *percentage outcomes*. John's price objection feels unique because this is a huge sale, and there is no "percentage outcome." This is a not a situation where holding my price might work some of the time, and sometimes not. It's all or nothing.

Abe would not agree because he would see this as one opportunity of many. If he were here right now, I know he'd be telling me to trust the process. He'd be telling me that I can use this moment to test the idea of holding my price. He might alternatively suggest I use one of the negotiation tactics he taught me.

This is a perfect moment to employ his "conditional offer" negotiation technique where you offer a price reduction contingent on a reciprocal concession. In my mind's fictitious debate with Abe, I consider this option while equally conceding this is also a moment to possibly hold my price. On the other hand, I tell him in my mind, I could just as easily put my best price on the table to avoid future regret of losing the sale today.

I have the authority to reduce my price as much as 2% to earn the sale and still make a tidy commission and rationalize a decent profit for the company. The internal voice advocating for a price concession takes charge and secretly suggests I utilize that authority to offer 2%. I would add the phrase "and nothing more" to show I can be a tough negotiator too.

That would be my way of drawing a line in the sand. It would allow me to justify in my mind and boast in the office that I "won" the negotiation, but I know that is delusion. Nevertheless, I would save face and that tidy boost to my income urges me to take the easy route. I'll be the hero to John and win a sale for my company. The problem is that a two percent concession would cost many thousands of profit dollars in the coming years.

As this last thought is sweeping through the list of negotiation options in my brain, it dawns on me that two percent might not even get the sale. Perhaps I should ask how much he meant when he said the price is a "little" too high. Perhaps I should remind him that the service value my company provides justifies my price. Perhaps I should tell him how committed I will be to his success as his "unpaid employee."

The options and scenarios snap through my brain like a pinball at lightspeed. What do I do?

2

It's a Million Points

"Your employer is your #1 customer," Abe said months earlier while we lunched at a sports-themed restaurant chain.

It sounds strange even now because the statement is counterintuitive. Most salespeople believe the most important customer they have is the one they sell *to*. Abe assured me that my most important customer is the one I sell *for*.

"Who is paying you?" Abe asked just when an energetic young waitress named Emily came to take our order. As he often does, Abe charmed her by asking a few questions about her life and complimenting her before we ordered and handed back our plastic-coated menus. The stale aroma of accumulated alcohol on wood was present because we were the first diners for lunch. The sports screens were silent but flickering with game replays and agitated talk show pundits. Abe seemed oblivious to it all and concentrated fully on the lesson he would deliver.

"Acme," I said plainly, before quickly adding, "*and* my customer. Well, I mean the product buyer. If I don't bring in customers, then there is no money to pay me with. Therefore, my job is to bring customers to Acme, right?"

Abe nodded and agreed before surprising me by saying that the companies to whom I sell are really Acme's customers. "You are the middleman. The buyer pays Acme. Acme pays you. Your job is to bring profitable clients to Acme. The client is their customer. You are the conduit. Therefore, Acme pays you not to bring just any customers, but to bring profitable ones."

"I'm not sure I see the distinction. I'm part of the company, so the buyer would at least be a shared customer with me and the company," I said.

"The company pays you to sell, yes?" Abe asked and I nodded.

"Good," he said. "Now, let's say you bring in a customer that seems profitable, but ends up costing the company more in service and problems than profits. You still get paid, but does the company really get value for your services if it loses money on an account?"

I told Abe that I try to get as much as I can for each sale. He smiled, not just because he knew I had often lowered my price when encountering the most casual resistance, but because I sounded like every young salesman he mentored before me. I conceded there were times I had lowered my price, but only because I knew where I had to be.

Abe was kind enough at that moment not to point out that every salesperson who ever lowered their price was able to justify the necessity of it in their minds, because they "knew where they had to be." Instead, he asked, "What about the sale to Image Builders? Remember that one?"

He was reminding me of a sale I had made after agreeing to a steep price concession. I later discovered the delivery was to a remote location, which cost the company excess processing time, gas, and the lost use of a truck for local, more routine deliveries. The situation got worse when we discovered that the buyer expected small deliveries with unanticipated frequency. We ultimately lost money on the deal and future business opportunities with Image Builders.

I had not asked the right questions prior to taking the order. More than likely, a competitor had done so and priced the project properly. That competitor ended up losing to a salesman who lowballed the bid because he didn't understand the situation and won the job at an undervalued price. That salesman was me.

"I know," I said sheepishly. "I still feel badly about that one."

"Why?" Abe asked before casually sipping his iced tea. "You lost an account that wasn't profitable. They created a lot of headaches."

"Yeah, I know," I admitted. I was relieved that Abe did not blame me for the lost business, but then walked into a trap. "Anyway," I said, "I lost a lot of income, too, when we lost that business."

As soon the words emerged, I realized the contradiction of my own statement and quickly acknowledged the mistake. It implied I was expecting to be paid on business that was unprofitable to my employer. Abe of course didn't let the subject drop.

"That's exactly my point," he said. "If you make money while Acme loses, what benefit is provided? Our job is to strive always to *increase* prices, and therefore profits, rather than lower them in negotiations. Acme relies on us and is our customer."

"I agree with that," I said, even though we both obviously knew my aforementioned lack of negotiation skills failed to match my stated beliefs. I had often called Abe to ask for price concessions which meant, in essence, I was negotiating on behalf of the buyer. I was representing the customer *to* Acme rather than negotiating as an advocate of profits *for* Acme.

"The day you lost Image Builders, do you remember what you did?" Abe asked me.

I laughed, because I remember Abe's exact words afterwards, when he told me, "You better work to replace that business. It's the only solution to the problem." I started prospecting that day.

"Losing that account was one of the best things you've ever done for your customer, Acme. That led to the sale with Beeline Builders, one of your most profitable accounts, and replaced the lost business of Image Builders with a better account." Beeline Builders remains a loyal and profitable customer today.

"I remember my first phone call to Charlie from Beeline. It was easy to get a meeting and eventually the sale," I told Abe. "It took about eight phone calls to other prospects that resulted in hang-ups, voice mails, and rejections before getting the meeting with Charlie. I'll never forget when he said, 'Your timing is perfect. We're in a bind and my current supplier is not getting it done.'"

I remember thinking to myself that it took a lot of effort and rejection to have so-called perfect timing. Abe assured me, "A salesperson should periodically hear they have perfect timing. It means they are prospecting enough to be in the right spot at the right time." Then he asked, "Do you believe in love at first sight?"

I laughed, not at his question, but the timing. I couldn't understand why he was asking me about love at first sight, so I said, "I guess. Yes, for some people. Yes."

Abe said, "Believe in *sale* at first sight, too. In real estate the three laws of success are location, location, location. If you have the right location with a lot of traffic, business comes easy. In sales the three laws are locate, locate, and locate. Find the opportunities with easy buyers who are happy to pay your price for good service. Then selling will be easy. That's what happened with Beeline Builders. The biggest obstacle to the price objection is not overcoming it, but instead finding the right buyer who won't even raise it."

"Sometimes you start a conversation with a prospect that feels right. There is an instant connection and intuition that things are going to work out. Have you had other customers besides Beeline Builders that fit that description?"

I watched Abe take a bite of his salad and thought about a few customers who made business easy right from the outset. I listed them and Abe said, "That, my friend, is sale at first sight. Selling doesn't always have to be forced persuasion and, in fact, probably shouldn't be. A good sales relationship usually feels right at the outset."

We ate our lunch in silence for a few moments. Televisions continued flickering as the waitstaff zoomed by our table. Seats filled up along with the noise of conversations and the clang of dishes. Abe focused our dialogue on sales theories. He says we should talk about sales in between calls to analyze our performance. "It's what professionals do…if they're serious about winning," he likes to say.

As the sports highlights ran, it reminded me of the time Abe joked that great baseball players and football players talk about baseball and football when they're on the sidelines between their performances on the field. They are in the game and concentrating on winning. Therefore, they talk about skills, maneuvers, and ways to compete against their current opponent.

"Do you know what salespeople talk about between sales calls?" he asked to set up his joke, before answering his own question. "Baseball and football! They should talk about the performance of their *sales* game between plays. Plays are to the game score as sales calls are to the profit score. Salespeople should discuss sales, not sports.

"For example, what if I told the owner of Acme that salespeople shouldn't be allowed to negotiate prices?" he asked as the means to start a conceptual sales dialogue.

I responded defensively and blurted, "I think that would be a huge mistake, a real error that would cost the company lots of money." I was flustered, like many salespeople would be. We consider ourselves competent negotiators and don't take lightly implications to the contrary.

"So," Abe asked calmly while gently pushing away his plate after swallowing the last bite of cobb salad, "what if I had…and what if the owner agreed? Then what? Hmmm? What would that mean for salespeople?"

"Um… Well…" I thought about it while Abe waited for my answer. I was unprepared and admitted, "I'm not sure."

Abe was relentless. He decided to share with me the truth about profit and loss statements. "Got any idea how much pre-tax profit our company makes?" he asked.

I knew that my gross product margins hovered near 24% so I made a wild guess and said, "Probably close to 10%."

"Nope," he said casually. "Try half of that. We earn 5% of the total sale, and that is during a decent year. "So, if you give away 1% of the price, how much does the company lose?"

"Are you asking how much is 1% of 5%?" I asked.

"Yep. That's exactly the math. So how much is it?" Abe asked.

"I guess, if you base it on those numbers, it would be 20% of the profit," I admitted reluctantly, while silently recognizing times I offered as much as 2% to get a sale and had considered offering more.

"Are there other numbers you and I *should* base it on?" he asked. It was a fair question. I paused and tried to rationalize a retort. Based on the information he gave me, however, there was nothing left but to agree.

"So, my question stands," Abe continued. "What would it mean if the company said you could no longer negotiate prices?"

"I think the company would be making a big mistake," I said overconfidently, without having an argument to justify my position. I knew what Abe wanted me to say. He wanted me to say that Acme wouldn't have to worry about a salesperson like me giving away 20-40% of the profits to make a sale, but I wasn't seeing it his way. I figured, like most salespeople, that a smaller profit is better than no profit at all.

Abe nodded and waited. His calmness frustrated me. It was a silly question in my mind. Salespeople negotiate prices. It's part of the job.

After dealing with the internal debate and silence of my mentor, I finally said, "Well…*if I decided to stick with the company*, I guess I'd just give my customers prices. And I'd have to tell them there is no wiggle room."

"Interesting," Abe said. I realized I had implicitly threatened to quit the company and wondered if that was what Abe found interesting or some other aspect of my answer.

"I'm sure a lot would say, 'No sale.'" I assured Abe.

"I'm sure they would."

"So…we'd lose business. You agree?" I asked, feeling as if I were gaining momentum in the debate.

"We might," Abe conceded. "That's for sure."

"Then I'd have to start looking for a lot more prospects to find the ones who'd buy at a fixed price," I added combatively.

"Good!" Abe said. It hit me that my answer, however defiantly I provided it, was actually a positive outcome in his mind. "What else?" he asked.

"Well," I said, still agitated by the absurdity of Abe's question while absentmindedly proving his point. "I'd make darn sure my customers understood everything we do and why our pricing is where it is."

Abe smiled and I realized these were the answers he was fishing for. I calmed down and really started thinking about it. "I would probably quote less and make sure I was speaking to sincerely interested buyers."

"Excellent!" Abe said. "I agree, and you'd probably want to

figure out ways that you, personally, could make yourself worth a higher price than the competition too, yes?" Abe asked.

I agreed, even though I couldn't think of how…yet.

Reading my mind, Abe volunteered, "You could provide sales leads." Then he added, "Perhaps you could share ways that potential buyers could learn from experiences you have had with their competitors in the market. Maybe you could supply information that helps your customer reduce operating costs, or perhaps increase *their* sales margins. Hmmm? What do you think?

"So," Abe said, without waiting for answers to his questions. "One. You'd prospect more. Two. You'd do more research on your customers. Three. You'd make sure you're talking to the right people. Four. You'd probably bid less because you'd figure out which buyers are sincere, and which aren't. Five. You'd bring them ideas and resources to make their businesses better. Yes?"

I nodded and let his ideas churn in my head. Finally, I said, "You know, it wouldn't be necessary to take away negotiation privileges. I think I could do all that anyway, even if I were still allowed to negotiate prices."

Abe grinned, and I couldn't help but smile back. His guidance was always calm and paternal. His simple question pointed out *several things I probably should be doing anyway, whether or not I have the authority to lower my prices.*

"Q.E.D." Abe said.

"Q.E.D.?" I asked.

"Quod Erat Demonstrandum. It's Latin. It means 'the case was proven.' Mathematicians use the letters after completing proof of a theory. I wasn't trying to stop you from negotiating, merely trying to prove that our job is not purely to sell. Our job is to sell profitably." Abe paused and then asked, "Q.E.D.?"

Point taken. "Q.E.D."

Abe said, "By the way I didn't…"

"Didn't what?" I asked.

He said, "I didn't tell the owner of Acme that salespeople shouldn't be allowed to negotiate. I just wanted you think about it."

I laughed and said, "You told me you *did* tell the owner we shouldn't be allowed to negotiate."

Abe laughed and said, "Nope. I said, '*What if I had* told the owner…? I told you we should talk about sales ideas between calls and we just did!"

It was a good lesson. I considered what it might mean to my sales performance if I could no longer rely on the crutch of a lower price."

"That 'point' salespeople give away so freely," Abe said while using two fingers from each hand to make quotation marks, "doesn't seem like much until you multiply it a million times. Our annual sales are $100 million. It's not just a single percentage point. It's a million of them! $1,000,000."

Emily arrived with the bill. She asked if we enjoyed the meal and Abe said, after glancing at the bill, "It was delicious, Emily, and your service was impeccable. But I'd like to ask you a question. Is there any way you can do something about the price of the meal? It's a little expensive if you ask me. Can you do better?"

I was stunned, but not nearly as much as Emily. She stammered and finally asked Abe if he was serious. He grinned and waited. Emily stared at him and offered apologetically,

"I'm sorry. My manager isn't here, and I can't do that."

In the kindest manner possible, Abe asked, "Why not?"

"Why can't I change the price?" Emily asked, still reeling from the incongruity of Abe's question.

"Yes," Abe said. "Why?"

Emily thought for a moment and then finally said, "I don't have the authority to do that. I'm sorry."

Abe winked at me with a smile. He gave her his credit card and, not surprisingly, included a very generous 30% tip when signing off. Then he asked me, "So, I think our job is to treat our employer like a paying customer, a high paying one at that. What do you think?"

I looked into the eyes of my sagacious mentor, smiled, and said, "Q.E.D."

3

Dirty Water at the Mouth of the River

"The price objection is like dirty water at the mouth of the river," Abe said. "You can try cleaning up the debris and pollutants going into the ocean at the mouth of the river but will never succeed. Factory chemicals, boat oil, and litter continue flowing downstream to the mouth. It's a hopeless battle until you address the problems upstream. That's how the price objection works. You have to cope with the problem early in the sales process."

I heard these words, not as a lecture to me, but instead a tip to our prospect. Jessica Sanders owns a small home improvement company. She told Abe and me that her customers were always shopping price and then asked, "Noah, what are other companies like mine doing to combat the price objection?"

"I think they all say the same thing," I said. "Everyone thinks their competitor is lowering the price and ruining the market, but nobody thinks or confesses they are the ones doing it." I laughed because I found humor in my accurate statement. Abe glanced at me, smiled with raised eyebrows, and acknowledged I had made a valid point. Jessica smiled too, but still didn't have the answer she was seeking. That is when Abe started talking about dirty water at the mouth of the river.

He pulled out a piece of paper and scribbled one of his patented diagrams. He illustrated the point in the river where the price objection occurs and then said, while pointing to the dot at the left side of his curly line, "You start here. Your intentions are great to begin with. After all your preparation and dialogue leading up to your final price, someone tells you it is too high. It shouldn't be a surprise, but it is. The next thing you know you are ready to lower your price because you're not prepared. We could call it *negotiation ignorance*. This is really the question, right?"

Jessica was engrossed with Abe's ideas and stared at the paper. When she looked up, I expected her to be insulted by the term "negotiation ignorance." Abe recognized the risk and qualified his statement, while looking over his glasses at her, "Ignorance is not a measure of intelligence, of course. It's a matter of training and education." He was seated on the edge of his chair, leaning onto the opposing side of Jessica's desk with his hands resting on the paper, prepared to continue his lesson if he had a willing pupil.

Jessica said, "Yes. That's the perfect word for it. I'm

successful in my business, but I have never had sales training. I'm not stupid, just ignorant. I don't know what I'm supposed to do in that moment."

Abe persisted because he did have a willing pupil. I remember Abe telling me that you can't coach the unwilling and the biggest obstacle to personal growth is not the teacher. It's the student. It made sense and Jessica was a great example of a willing student. Abe said, "This is what happens next." He put another box on his diagram and wrote "lost profits!"

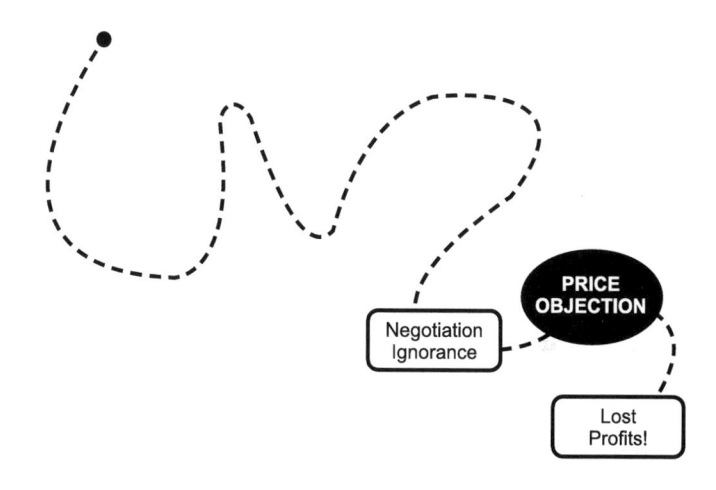

[Diagram: a squiggly dashed line leading to "Negotiation Ignorance" → "PRICE OBJECTION" → "Lost Profits!"]

Jessica nodded, looked at Abe and asked, "Great! So that's the problem. What am I supposed to do about that price objection? What do I say?"

Abe calmly suggested a lot of things probably went wrong early in the process with the homeowner. He asked Jessica to describe what happened leading up to that recent price objection. Jessica said that her prospect was a homeowner planning to renovate her kitchen. "Everything was going great until I delivered my price. The woman got cold feet and said she would have to think about it. So, I left my quote with her to review. Now I am afraid she might be sharing it with other remodelers bidding for her business."

Abe countered, "Or maybe she just has it in a desk drawer. Or maybe it is sitting on her kitchen counter. Maybe she is excited about hiring you and figuring out how to come up with the money." Abe shared these ideas as a means to help Jessica calm herself. He has used similar strategies on me many times. Jessica smiled and admitted that she was probably making the situation a lot worse in her mind than it was in reality.

Abe asked a few more questions to understand Jessica's pricing and bid process. We learned she had provided her buyer a project drawing, the list of materials, a dollar figure, and payment requirements. Nothing more. He asked her a few questions about the buyer. "What were the things most important to her when you discussed her kitchen prior to the quote?"

Jessica pointed out that the woman wanted modern appliances and a brighter kitchen. Then Jessica leaned back in her chair to ponder her conversations with the buyer. "She is obsessed about her dog. Um…Theodore! That's the dog's name."

Jessica wasn't a dog person and found strange her prospect's overzealous affection for a dog. "Theodore?" Abe asked while mirroring Jessica's behavior by leaning back in his chair.

"Yep. Theodore. She loves that dog. It's like a family member," Jessica said dismissively.

Abe listened and then said, "A kitchen remodel can be

a messy thing. I've been through it." Then he asked a few questions. "Did you mention in your proposal that you would need to turn the water off eventually? Or share that your customer might have to cook with a hotplate for a few days during the process? Did you describe all the things that usually affect a homeowner's lifestyle and how you shepherd customers comfortably through a remodeling project?"

Jessica admitted that none of those factors were included in her quote. Abe reminded Jessica that she remodels homes every day and that her customer does it once in a lifetime. "Maybe she needs your guidance," Abe suggested. "How many customers have you had in the past who were shocked by the inconveniences they suffered because nobody told them in advance."

"Almost all of them. There were a few arguments too, but no divorces…although a few came close," Jessica said with a laugh.

Abe laughed and said, "Ha! Maybe you should warn clients that disagreements are likely, but that none of your projects have resulted in divorce yet…unlike your competitors!"

Jessica was seeing how Abe's mind reshaped sales interactions. They both knew the subject of divorce was a joke, but not a complete joke. It would certainly amuse clients to hear the words and lighten the dialogue.

"Bring the future into the present," Abe said and then continued. "Thoughts about outcomes excite buyers. They only see the before and after picture on HGTV, Pinterest and other media, not the mess in between. You have to help them get from point A to point B. The education that prepares the buyer for a major home renovation project really elevates the salesperson's credibility. And there's more…

"Thoughts of the future release powerful brain chemicals that produce happiness and optimism. In the moments when you discuss outcomes, you are already dispelling concerns about your price compared to competitors. You are differentiating yourself and, instead of figuring out ways to shop, buyers are already rationalizing why they want to do business with you."

Jessica looked at Abe and repeated his words, "*Bring the future into the present.* That is really great. Nearly every time we do a project, there is excitement during the planning process and joy when it is all done. But during construction? Oh boy! Unexpected inconveniences create tension because clients are surprised at the mess, or length of time it takes, or delays caused by changes. These things aren't surprises to me, but they are to them. Bringing their future into the present is a great concept."

Abe nodded and let Jessica's voice tail off. After a brief moment of quiet, Abe asked the surprise question, "So where did you mention Theodore's safety during the construction process in your proposal?"

Jessica chuckled. "I didn't," she admitted. "And I guarantee you that, if I had, she would have been thrilled to see that. Instead, I am sitting here explaining to my partners why we don't have the sale we need for a spring project."

"So, did you lower the price?" Abe asked as further investigation.

"No. Not yet anyway. We're looking at the numbers."

Abe added three new boxes to his drawing. "This means we have a proposal with *incomplete information* provided. You are feeling *management pressure* from your partners. And, as far as I can tell, you haven't done much to distinguish yourself from the other remodelers in the market. You haven't gone beyond *commodity credibility*.

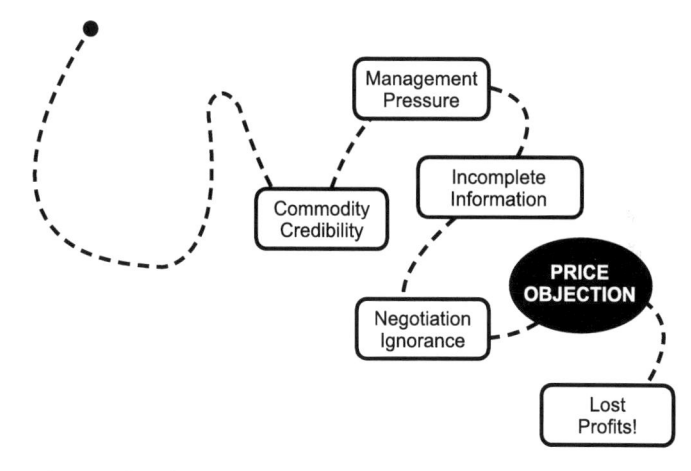

Diagram: A dashed path leads from a starting point through "Commodity Credibility," "Management Pressure," "Incomplete Information," and "Negotiation Ignorance" to "PRICE OBJECTION," ending at "Lost Profits!"

Jessica let those words ring in her ear. She asked the same question I was thinking. "What is 'commodity credibility'?"

Abe said, "Buyers can purchase the brands you and I sell from a lot of people. Your granite countertops are mere commodities. The doors and windows you buy come from a local vendor that also supplies your competitors. In fact, most of your competitors sell the same products and outsource from identical suppliers, yes?"

Jessica was looking at Abe's diagram before looking up and nodding, "Yes," she said. "That's true."

Abe continued, "If we don't give our customers a reason to buy from us other than providing a readily available commodity at a price, our credibility is no greater than the commodity itself. We could call that commodity credibility. Make sense?"

Jessica nodded. I could tell she was impressed with Abe. Heck, I was too! I had no idea where all this was coming from because, in the months I had worked with him, he had never shared the diagram.

"You could go beyond the level of commodity credibility in one sentence," he said. Then he paused. Jessica waited with anticipation as did I! It was a tactic of Abe's to make students think about answers to questions. If they had the answers, he was happy to praise them. If they didn't, he wanted them to be aware of the learning moment by removing any opportunity for them to say the already knew the answer. Clearly neither Jessica nor I had the answer.

"You could put in your proposal a section that includes 'Key Issues' and write, 'Theodore's comfort is essential, and we should discuss a safety plan for him during construction.'"

Jessica smiled and said, "I love that! I bet it would do a lot to improve my chances!"

Abe added that she could include a lot more in the "Key Issues" section about product selection and deadlines the buyer should meet; your scheduling plan; things to expect like temporary lifestyle inconveniences; how the new brighter kitchen with modern appliances will increase the home value; and other considerations. He reminded Jessica of the tension she has observed with families during remodeling projects and how she counsels them to avoid that tension. Abe took to his sheet again and added a few more boxes to his river path of "dirty water."

"Do you have a clear pricing policy that includes accounting for your labor, equipment, marketing expenses, and other burden to your company?" he asked. "You just said you're 'looking at the numbers,' which tells me you have a lot of pricing flexibility, or at least uncertainty, in your policies."

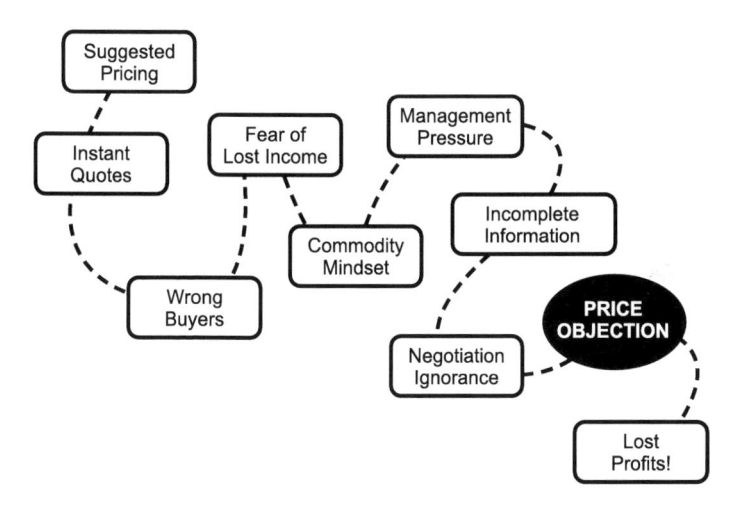

```
                Suggested
                 Pricing
                    |
                    |
    Instant     Fear of      Management
    Quotes    Lost Income     Pressure
        \       /    \         /
         \     /      \       /
          \   /        \     /      Incomplete
           \ /          \   /       Information
            X            \ /
           / \         Commodity
          /   \         Mindset
     Wrong                          PRICE
     Buyers                        OBJECTION
                    Negotiation
                    Ignorance
                                    Lost
                                   Profits!
```

Jessica said her company's pricing was based on a standard markup to fixed expenses and product costs. She then admitted they were almost always willing to negotiate. Abe retorted quickly, "We call that *suggested pricing* because it's not really what you expect to get. It's not a price; it's a starting point that you're willing to negotiate under pressure, yes?"

Jessica agreed and Abe asked, "Why?"

"Why what?"

"Why are you so willing to negotiate?" Abe asked. Of course, he knew the answer, but wanted Jessica to discover it for herself.

Jessica smiled and let her finger touch the paper and point to the words *fear of lost income*. Abe pursed his lips, touched his chin with an index finger, and furrowed his brow, the way he often did when deep in thought. "I wrote the words *instant quotes* too," he said. "I wrote those words because I know that Noah has done it. I've done it. At some point we all do it. How about you? I'm wondering if you do it too, sometimes."

Jessica sat back in her chair. The grin she gave Abe intimated full trust in him. "Have you been spying on me?" she asked. "It's amazing how many times we get shoppers who give us plans or vague ideas of their remodeling dreams without detail. We price a lot of those and discover we're not even close to the buyer's expectations. So, yes, we end up doing a lot of extra work because we price projects with incomplete information." Jessica paused and concluded, "Yep. We give *instant quotes*."

Abe said, "Consider what you just said. You get shoppers who give you vague details and cost you excessive time when they aren't prepared to invest the time in their own project planning. Those might be the *wrong buyers*. Maybe you need better ones."

Jessica looked at me said, "Noah, you better stick around this guy. I think he can teach you a lot of things." Then she looked at Abe and said, "Can I keep that piece of paper?"

Abe smiled and leaned back, "Sure, but only if you'll make a couple copies for Noah and me."

Jessica blinked in surprise and asked, "Don't you already have this written down somewhere?"

Abe said, "Truthfully, I never thought this much about it. I always liked to say that the price objection is like dirty water at the mouth of the river, but I never got into this much detail. I think there is a lot here to think about!"

Jessica agreed. She made copies and walked us to the front

door of her showroom. She thanked us and said, "You just solidified your position as our supplier of windows. Thank you so much for your help!"

Abe provided Jessica a sales and marketing lesson that would deflect any future price objection. He made her a client long before the first transaction by establishing credibility. "The relationship comes before the transaction," Abe says. He assures me we prove the value we will deliver after the first transaction by providing value before it. In a five-minute presentation, he simultaneously described and demonstrated the power of consultative credibility.

In the car I thanked Abe for helping me land a new account. I told him that his theory is really great. "It is true that you just made that up in her office?" I asked.

I was surprised when Abe said, "Yes and no. It is true that I have talked about the idea of dirty water, but just as a clever saying. I've never really labeled all the obstacles we encounter during our journey to the sale until now. Discussing the process with Jessica reveals some universal truths about selling." He was staring at the diagram he had just created while ideas circulated in his head. "I feel like we've only identified the problem," he said while folding the paper and sliding it into the inner pocket of his blazer. "Let's get to work solving it."

4

Established Pricing

Abe and I returned to the office after our meeting with Jessica in the late afternoon. He led me into the "bullpen." This is the work room he set up exclusively for our sales team. It is well lit and furnished with a utilitarian conference table and enough electronics for the room to be highly functional but not fancy. Abe wanted a place where salespeople could work but not get so comfortable that we neglected getting out to the field. We go there to review blueprints, meet with customers, and hold team meetings. He likes to call it the bullpen because it is where we prepare for battle, like pitchers before they go out to the baseball mound.

I expected his usual tips for the end of a coaching session. "Coaching sessions" are what he calls his days in the field with me. At the end of each day, he gives me some tips to progressively build my skills and confidence. Today was different.

Abe was thinking intensely about his new sales theory. He pulled out his diagram and looked at it. He asked me what I thought about it. I told him it made a lot of sense. He obviously saw something vitally important about his theory and said, "I think every single box on this diagram has a story, each of which has a key to overcoming the price objection."

He circled his first box where he had written *suggested pricing* and softly said, "starting points." Then he turned to me and asked, "Do you remember when I said to Jessica that she was delivering 'starting points?'"

"Yes. I thought that was an interesting comment. What does it mean?"

He looked to me and said, "If every price we deliver is negotiable, then it really is nothing more than a starting point. I said before that it's an asking price."

"Isn't that what everyone tries to get in sales?" I asked. "Their asking price?"

"Yes," Abe conceded, "which is exactly the problem. Why are we asking? Don't we know? Are we unsure what our prices should be? If we are, then why don't we just have everyone tell us where our price ought to be or how much they *feel* like paying?"

I thought about Abe's sardonic words and volunteered, "It's like an asking price is encouraging the buyer to negotiate."

"Exactly!" Abe said. You could see he was onto a thought and wanted to prove something. "We need to start delivering *'telling'* prices.'"

"What's a telling price?" I asked.

"It's a *price*," Abe said flatly. "It's not a starting point.

It's not an *asking* price. It is what we expect to be paid. The problem is we start out never expecting to get our price in the first place. Our customer isn't negotiating with us. We're negotiating with ourselves."

He sat next to me at the conference table. He opened his computer to upload a pricing report, sorted by customer, and turned the computer to face me.

"Look," Abe said. I stared at the spreadsheet he created. It was my year-to-date pricing report. Abe said, "These are your customers and the pricing levels you're getting. I purposely took out the names of customers so you could just see the numeric trend. What do you see?"

I looked at the list and commented about the overall sales margin, which was a respectable 24%, or at least close. Abe said, "Look closer. Look at the individual pricing patterns."

I stared, then looked up and down the sheet. "I don't really see any clear pattern. It looks like the pricing is pretty random," I concluded.

"That's it!" Abe said. "There *isn't* a pattern. Your largest volume customer buys at a 23% margin and the next, a pretty large account is at 19.5%. Your third largest is higher than both. What does this tell you?"

BEAT THE PRICE OBJECTION

Noah Foster Annual Sales

Volume Rank	Cost of Goods	Sales Volume	Margin %	Margin Dollars
1	$ 283,529	$ 368,220	23.0%	$ 84,691
2	200,130	248,609	19.5%	48,479
3	111,119	148,555	25.2%	37,436
4	45,423	68,521	33.7%	23,098
5	49,684	65,202	23.8%	15,518
6	36,490	47,084	22.5%	10,594
7	30,242	40,216	24.8%	9,974
8	28,664	35,608	19.5%	6,944
9	16,730	22,949	27.1%	6,219
10	16,482	20,628	20.1%	4,146
11	10,196	17,983	43.3%	7,787
12	8,121	11,527	36.1%	4,161
13	5,096	6,833	28.2%	1,927
14	4,757	5,887	19.2%	1,130
15	2,911	2,985	40.3%	1,203
16	2,314	2,614	9.9%	259
Totals	$ 851,889	$ 1,113,421	23.7%	$ 263,565

I started to feel a little embarrassed because anyone could plainly see my pricing made no sense. I knew who the top customers were and was unsure of a few near the bottom, except the last one. As fortune would have it, Abe asked, "Do you know who bought that small order from you at a 9.9% margin?"

"It was a guy named Tony Capaccio who works for a window replacement company. He was doing a job for his aunt and wanted a good price. He also told me he might start his own business one day, so I wanted to make sure he remembered me if he ever did."

Established Pricing   37

We talked about Tony for a moment and the multitude of implications about my pricing strategy. Abe got me to reveal a lot, most notably that Tony works for a customer of ours, Forthright Construction, that one of our other salespeople, Evan Keller, handles. "I'm happy that neither Evan nor Tony's employer found out about this," Abe said before asking, "What if Tony's employer found out you had given Tony a far better deal than Forthright Construction gets? What if Evan found out? If Tony had asked Evan for a price, what price would Evan have offered?"

Abe waited for an answer to his last question until I conceded, "He probably would have priced at a level higher than he sells Forthright Construction to avoid any problems with his bigger account."

Abe talked quickly when his mind was processing information like this. "Think about the implications of that sale for a moment and your reasons for pricing so differently than you expect Evan might have. You got caught up worrying about other suppliers in the market. This sale proves that sometimes the very competitor we fear is the salesman inside our own head…or our own company. Who knows? Maybe Tony called someone else in our company and got a higher price that he didn't like, then called back and got you."

Strangely, Abe wasn't being judgmental. He was being critical. "*Critical* is a word I love," Abe once said with a smile. "Most people presume that criticism must include judgments of good or bad, right or wrong. I think we can be critical of our performance without pejoratives."

It could have been embarrassing that I sacrificed so much profit on a small sale, but Abe let it pass. It was true, however.

I had made a big pricing mistake without considering for a moment the implications it had to the bigger picture of my company's business. Abe asked me, truly to understand my thought process, "What were you feeling when you gave Tony such a low price?"

After consideration, I confessed, "I'm not sure. Maybe it felt like such a small sale that a lower price wouldn't matter, which I now realize is wrong." After a little more thought, I admitted, "Fear. I guess I was just afraid of losing a sale. I felt like he was shopping a price to see if we were competitive, and I wanted to make sure I got the order."

"So," Abe said. He paused and thought about the sales mindset before saying, "A buyer requests a price and the first thing we think as salespeople is, 'oh no! this buyer wants to see if I'm competitive. We don't stop to think that they aren't negotiating. In *their* minds, they are just asking for the price they will have to pay. In *our* minds, we hear a negotiation even though there never was one. They're simply asking, 'How much is it?' Instead, we hear, 'what is the best you can do?'"

I confessed, "That is exactly what happened with me. He asked me how much it would be for six units, and I panicked. I assumed he wanted to know if I was competitive. It never occurred to me that he might only have wondered if his credit card had a high enough limit. That was stupid of me."

Abe waived off my self-denigration. "Don't be silly," he said. "This is what *everyone* does. You're not alone. Your pricing matrix is likely consistent across our entire company. We're trying to fix the problem, not blame you or anyone. Let's call it 'opinion pricing.' Salespeople fear a negotiation and then figure they have the right opinion, although without evidence, where the price should be."

Abe was more captivated by his new "dirty water" theory than he was about my personal performance. The spreadsheet illustrated bigger, organizational problems. A buyer could get a price and, if they didn't like it, hang up the phone and call back to easily get another salesperson *at the same company* who might offer a better price for an identical product. In other words, if they didn't get the desired "opinion" about a price from one salesperson, maybe the next one would give it to them.

Crazy? Yes. Unrealistic? No. It has happened and, if a buyer can get different prices from the same company, it would mean we were competing against ourselves. I thought about all the implications of arbitrary pricing and fear-based negotiations while Abe typed at his laptop. He left me waiting while he worked, another habit of his. He didn't mind putting in the work to help others but expected them to invest time with him. He only coached willing pupils and truth be told, in that moment, I was forcing my will to learn. Sometimes the lessons hurt my pride, if not my brain.

Abe broke my thoughts by excitedly saying, "Noah! Remember that little conversation we had in the restaurant? Remember when I asked, 'What if you weren't allowed to negotiate?' Look!"

He showed me the same spreadsheet, but this time with additional columns that illustrated the implications of a fixed pricing matrix. The conclusions were obvious.

Noah Foster Annual Sales — What If…

Volume Rank	Cost of Goods	Sales Volume	Margin %	Margin Dollars	Adjusted Volume	Margin %	Margin Dollars
1	$ 283,529	$ 368,220	23.0%	$ 84,691	$ 373,065	24.0%	$ 89,536
2	200,130	248,609	19.5%	48,479	263,329	24.0%	63,199
3	111,119	148,555	25.2%	37,436	146,209	24.0%	35,090
4	45,423	68,521	33.7%	23,098	60,563	25.0%	15,141
5	49,684	65,202	23.8%	15,518	66,245	25.0%	16,561
6	36,490	47,084	22.5%	10,594	48,653	25.0%	12,163
7	30,242	40,216	24.8%	9,974	40,323	25.0%	10,081
8	28,664	35,608	19.5%	6,944	38,219	25.0%	9,555
9	16,730	22,949	27.1%	6,219	22,306	25.0%	5,577
10	16,482	20,628	20.1%	4,146	21,976	25.0%	5,494
11	10,196	17,983	43.3%	7,787	14,566	30.0%	4,370
12	8,121	11,527	36.1%	4,161	12,494	35.0%	4,373
13	5,096	6,833	28.2%	1,927	7,840	35.0%	2,744
14	4,757	5,887	19.2%	1,130	7,318	35.0%	2,561
15	2,911	2,985	40.3%	1,203	4,478	35.0%	1,567
16	2,314	2,614	9.9%	259	3,560	35.0%	1,246
Totals	$ 851,889	$ 1,113,421	23.7%	$ 263,565	$ 1,131,147	24.7%	$ 279,258

"What if we structured margins to align with categories of volume purchases or other criteria?" he asked.

He wasn't pushing a lesson as much as asking my honest viewpoint. I noted, "The added spreadsheet columns prove that a structured pricing matrix would increase margins by 1%. That's pretty cool."

"It increases our margins by 1%, yes, but what does it do to our profitability?!" he asked excitedly.

I sat waiting for him to finish his thought while staring at me with a smile. He was animated, the way he gets when he is learning something with you. It's as though he isn't teaching, but really just wants a fellow student to keep up. He waited for my answer until he finally raised his eyebrows and bobbled his head around as if to say, "Well, dummy? What is it?!"

Of course, Abe would never call me a dummy. But I felt like one in that moment because I didn't get the answer and, finally, it hit me! "Wow. You mean how much of a *profit increase* is it?"

"Yes. Yes," Abe said, waiting for me to acknowledge the significant implication.

"Well…if we make 5% profit like you said, then 1% more would be a 20% increase…which is $1,000,000 for the company. Wow."

"So, what do you think?" he asked now that he had proven his point. "Do you think we should have *suggested* pricing or *established* pricing parameters based on merit?" He wasn't really looking for an answer from me, but instead thinking out loud. He always liked to say, "You can't 'invent' a sales process. It is something to be *revealed*." In this moment, he was revealing truths about pricing practices that were flawed.

It is pretty obvious when you look at the numbers, but something salespeople and organizations manage to ignore or rationalize, if they bother at all to analyze pricing data. Abe said, "A few clicks of a pen and a wise decision could make a huge difference in profits while customers wouldn't flinch for a second. In fact, it might be the right thing to do for their confidence in our pricing."

"What do you mean by merit?" I asked. "…like the better a salesperson proves they can negotiate, the more latitude they get?"

"No," Abe said. "Customer merit. Pricing should be based on volume, loyalty, and the cost of doing business. We might not have exact calculations, but should at least be thinking about these factors."

Abe paused for a moment and then started clicking his keyboard. "What if..." he said, while clicking away at his keyboard. He popped a new image on the screen and turned his computer to me.

"If we nudged our pricing up just a little, we could increase profits a lot." His new pricing analysis showed a way to increase margins by 2%, translating to an increase in profits by 40%!

"Do you think a small customer who walks in to buy only a few windows would balk at a slightly higher price?" he asked before answering his own question. "I don't. I think we fear the price negotiation more than our customers do.

"We hand our prices to buyers with overt signals that tell them we expect to negotiate. We say things like, 'Here is my price sheet. Let me know where we stand.' Or we ask, 'Does that put us in the ballpark?' We hand people prices with unsure gestures and subliminal messages that are invitations to negotiate."

Established Pricing 43

Volume Rank	Cost of Goods	Sales Volume	Margin %	Margin Dollars	Adjusted Volume	Margin %	Margin Dollars
	Noah Foster Annual Sales				What If…		
1	$ 283,529	$ 368,220	23.0%	$ 84,691	$ 378,039	25.0%	$ 94,510
2	200,130	248,609	19.5%	48,479	266,840	25.0%	66,710
3	111,119	148,555	25.2%	37,436	148,159	25.0%	37,040
4	45,423	68,521	33.7%	23,098	60,563	25.0%	15,141
5	49,684	65,202	23.8%	15,518	66,245	25.0%	16,561
6	36,490	47,084	22.5%	10,594	48,653	25.0%	12,163
7	30,242	40,216	24.8%	9,974	40,323	25.0%	10,081
8	28,664	35,608	19.5%	6,944	40,949	30.0%	12,285
9	16,730	22,949	27.1%	6,219	23,900	30.0%	7,170
10	16,482	20,628	20.1%	4,146	23,545	30.0%	7,064
11	10,196	17,983	43.3%	7,787	14,566	30.0%	4,370
12	8,121	11,527	36.1%	4,161	11,601	30.0%	3,480
13	5,096	6,833	28.2%	1,927	7,280	30.0%	2,184
14	4,757	5,887	19.2%	1,130	7,928	40.0%	3,171
15	2,911	2,985	40.3%	1,203	4,852	40.0%	1,941
16	2,314	2,614	9.9%	259	3,857	40.0%	1,543
Totals	$ 851,889	$ 1,113,421	23.7%	$ 263,565	$ 1,147,302	25.7%	$ 295,413

"We don't deliver prices. We deliver starting points when we should be telling the customer our fair price with confidence." Abe paused and stared at me, then asked, "As you look at this pricing analysis, Noah, what do *you* think we should do?"

I was pretty certain that Abe was now making a case for a standard pricing policy that previously, during lunch, had only been a theoretical construct to prove a point. My mind wandered to the 18 other outside salespeople and eight inside sales representatives. I wondered how they would react to Abe's idea before reluctantly accepting it by saying, "I guess this means we probably should have a standard pricing policy and eliminate the authority for salespeople to negotiate."

"You do?" Abe asked. He was genuinely surprised. "You don't think there are times to negotiate?"

He was always confusing me. Like almost any sales representative, I wanted to have negotiation authority and I told him so. He quickly responded, "That's an interesting term you just shared. *Negotiation authority.* I think that is really the problem. It's not whether or not you actually have the authority. It's whether or not the buyer knows.

"If the buyer believes you have no authority to negotiate, then the price is no longer a starting point delivered reluctantly. They realize that someone else is in charge of pricing decisions and the salesperson is relieved of the burden. It's a price that your customers recognize is applied with consistency!"

Abe said those last words by landing his index finger firmly on the conference room table. The fit, grey-haired man just loved talking about sales theory. His passion was contagious and the more I was around him, the more I wanted to learn about sales. He asked, "What is more powerful for you as a salesperson? Is it better to have negotiation authority or not?"

"It's definitely more powerful to have it," I said.

Abe quickly disagreed. "Remember when I asked our waitress, Emily, for a better deal on lunch. She couldn't fathom lowering her price because she had no authority. This secured profit for the restaurant and gave her power to hold the price. Negotiation authority is illusory power. It enables salespeople to lower prices but denies them the ability to tell customers those prices were set in stone by an employer.

"Negotiation leverage is out of your hands. Therefore, your buyer has to give you a reason to negotiate on their behalf and, because you are not authorized to reduce your price, this consequently puts you in a more powerful position to hold it. If you don't have negotiation authority, then you deliver prices with finality. You deliver telling prices. End of story."

"I'm confused," I said. "This means you think salespeople should or shouldn't negotiate?"

Abe walked to the whiteboard in our bullpen and recreated his diagram that showed the dirty water at the mouth of the river. This time, he boldly outlined the source of the river and replaced the words *suggested pricing* and wrote in a dark color, **Established Pricing**.

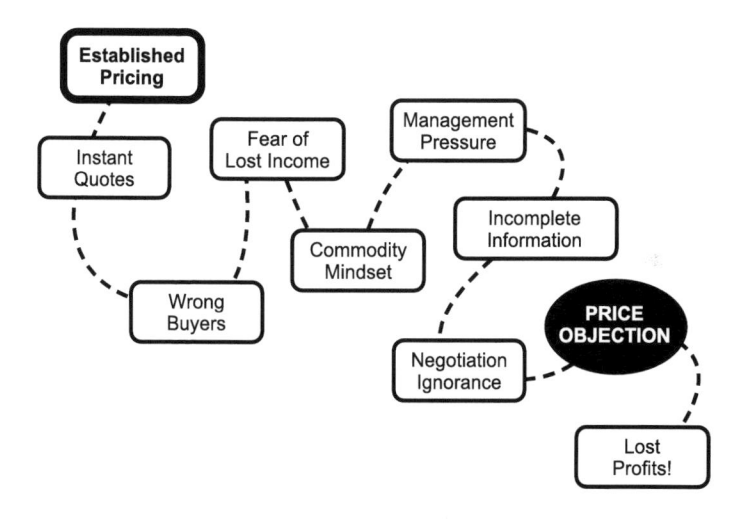

[Diagram: **Established Pricing** flows to Instant Quotes, Fear of Lost Income, and Management Pressure, which connect through Wrong Buyers, Commodity Mindset, Incomplete Information, and Negotiation Ignorance to **PRICE OBJECTION**, leading to Lost Profits!]

Then he looked back at me and said, "We're not talking about should or shouldn't. We're talking about perception and performance. It's less important whether or not you have negotiation authority and more important that you deliver a price with the belief it is your final offer. We're talking about *believing* in your price and delivering it as fair-trade value for products and services tendered. Negotiations become the exception rather than the rule," he concluded.

"Don't you think we'll lose sales from holding too firm on prices?" I asked.

"Some, yes," Abe conceded. "That's why I asked you at lunch what would happen if you no longer could negotiate. What would it force you to do?" It made me think of all the things I listed like prospecting more; doing more research; providing ideas to help my customers profit; pricing less reactively and with more information; and talking to the right people.

These elements of performance are now in the forefront of my consciousness. I want to shout at John and tell him he is being unreasonable, and it's obvious when you consider that I've done everything on that list. I have earned and deserve his business. Heck, it took my involvement with his customer to finalize window details. I got things right for him. John Henderson sits here waiting for my answer while implying my price is a starting point. His negotiation tactic presumes we don't have a sensible and fair pricing policy.

Strangely, this anger I feel seems better than being afraid, or at least I think it is. I can show John my skills too! I can tell John I do not have pricing authority and accept he might push back. This answer would at least buy me some time. In fact, I quickly decided that he actually does *not* know if I have pricing authority and therefore, in my mind, I will agree that I don't.

Nevertheless, if I tell him that I have no pricing authority, he will probably expect me to call someone who *does* have it. I can say that, but I think I have a better answer.

5

Speed is the Enemy of Profit

You might be thinking to yourself, "Of course Noah is going to hold his price. Why else would he be sharing his story?"

You might be right or might be wrong. The thing you should know is that, either way, it's important a customer feels great about the price. Did you ever stop to think about the implications of a price concession?

Abe illustrated the psychological power of small price concessions when he said, "A lot goes wrong in the mind of the buyer when a lower price is offered and accepted without justification."

"The first problem is that a precedent is set," Abe said.

"Your future prices are received as starting points. The moment you negotiate one price, you open the door to negotiate all of them.

"The larger problem is that the customer is left wondering why they had to ask. It's as if the first price, had they accepted it, would have been a mistake on their part. In other words, your original price (and you) had no credibility.

"The third problem is that you might leave the buyer wondering if they could have done better! Let's say you do get the sale after lowering your price one percent; the buyer is happy to 'win' the negotiation, but might later wonder, 'Hmmm…should I have gotten two or three percent? Did I really win or was I tricked?'"

Abe continued by softly noting, almost to himself, as if discovering the piece to a new puzzle, "There is a lot of psychology in the price negotiation. In fact, the only way a buyer knows they got your best price, if you really think about it, is if you draw a line in the sand." Abe insightfully added, "It's a natural feeling in any negotiation whether you are the buyer or seller. A quick concession potentially creates doubt about the exchange."

"The salesperson says, 'That's it. I promised my best price and you got it.' The salesperson might be scared and shaking on the inside while waiting for an answer, but it is the only way the buyer knows there is no wiggle room.

"Oh yes!" Abe added. "Even if you lower your price, there is no guarantee you will get the sale if you have negotiated improperly."

"What do you mean by 'negotiated improperly?'" I asked Abe.

"We'll get to that." he said. "For now, let's agree that a lot of things go wrong way upstream. The negotiation happens after the price objection. We have a lot of work to put in before we get to the actual negotiation. The key thought is that a buyer might not be fully satisfied psychologically if you do lower your price. You have to make them feel good about it. It must be justified in their minds."

I am in the actual negotiation and, if I lower my price for no reason, John will be left wondering if he could have done better and if I was being greedy at the start of our negotiation. While my proposal sits between us on John's desk, I am analyzing if I really need to lower my price. If I do, I'm trying to figure out how to make John still trust me and feel good about his purchase. I wonder if John is just testing the waters. Does he have another supplier waiting in the wings? Is it possible he only wants to see how low I will go before leveraging my price in a negotiation with another supplier?

My mind flashes through the process leading up to this moment. The first conversation I had with John allowed me to use Abe's "patented bid avoidance" technique. I remember the first time he had ever shared it with me. We had been talking about salespeople who give prices too eagerly.

Abe replaced the words *instant quotes* with the words **Bid Avoidance** on the graph of his evolving theory. It was another moment in Abe's selling game of puzzles. He once said, "It's a common move for buyers to ask you to bid on projects even though you don't have adequate information. You ask them to at least meet with you before your give them a price. They respond by telling you it is necessary for you to prove your competitive before they'll meet, yes?"

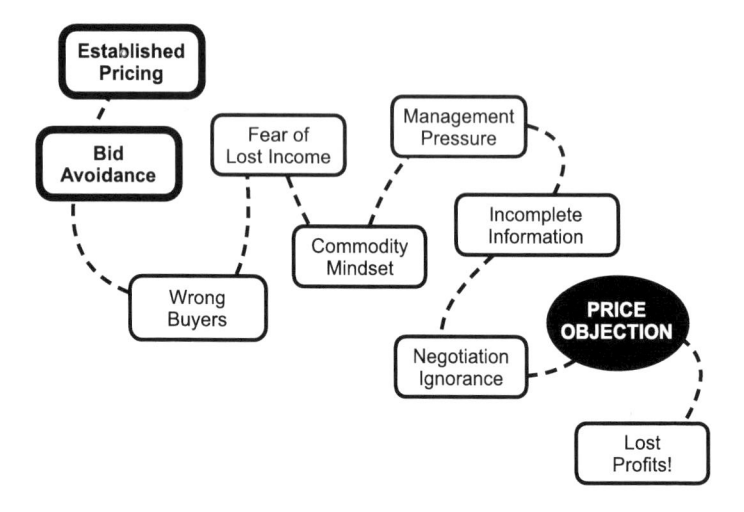

```
Established
  Pricing
     |
     ↓                                    Management
   Bid          Fear of                    Pressure
 Avoidance    Lost Income                     |
     \           |                            |
      \          |         Incomplete
       \         |         Information
        \     Commodity         |
         \    Mindset           |         PRICE
          \     |               |       OBJECTION
           Wrong                |            |
           Buyers           Negotiation      |
                            Ignorance        |
                                             ↓
                                           Lost
                                          Profits!
```

I nodded, but also didn't see many options. "If a buyer wants a price, but won't meet, what can I do?" I asked.

Abe said to me. "It's like a blind reverse auction when you play that game. The buyer asks you to price with minimal information. All your competitors are pricing to win, often based on the same limited information. Their instinct is to go lower, not higher like a traditional auction. Worse yet, the buyer is the only one who gets to see the bids, leaving you guessing in the blind. Make sense?"

I nodded because it did make sense. I thought about all the times I gave a buyer pricing and was told I was too high. I laughed and said, "I've never had a buyer show me a competitor's quote to help me raise my price nor ask me to do so. They hold the information and expect us to lower our price blindly without any evidence or reason."

Abe reminded me of the time a few days earlier when he said, "It's time for you to learn my *patented blind bid avoidance move*."

"The blind bid avoidance *move*?" I asked. We were driving to an appointment where I would be delivering a quote to Gary Allenby, a former prospect. Gary couldn't guarantee he would be available to meet but was eager for my price. He told me to drop it at his office and catch him when I arrived. I had invested over two hours to prepare a price for him and was excited about the opportunity.

Abe smiled placidly as if waiting and knowing what would happen in a matter of minutes. He knew the timing was ripe for the lesson I was about to receive. "Yep, the 'blind bid avoidance' move," he said. "A prospect calls you. Maybe you call them. You're anxious to meet and open a dialogue, but the buyer tells you to shoot them a price first. They promise to meet after you prove you're competitive. It's a common move, isn't it?"

This was the exact situation with the buyer I was headed to meet, and Abe senses it. He is setting me up for a vital learning lesson. I hadn't met Gary and agreed to provide a bid in hopes that my price would get my foot in the door. As we drove, I got that sinking feeling that occurs when you're with Abe. He knows and you don't. You hope he's wrong.

We entered the office and Jenny, a very kind young woman, greeted us. She told me that Gary was out. "He told me you'd be coming," Jenny said cheerily. "I assume you're dropping off your bid."

"I am," I said. Abe was standing silently next to me. During the drive, he had predicted my price would be treated as a bottom-line number and compared to many others without merit or any differentiating factors between suppliers. He predicted that I wouldn't likely get the business unless I came in significantly lower than Allenby's current supplier and lower than all the other competitors.

"If price is the only weapon you bring to the fight," he once advised, "then price is the only factor that matters."

"Maybe it would better if I tried to schedule time with Gary before leaving my price," I said to Jenny. She smiled and said that Gary probably won't meet unless we are really competitive. She convinced me that it was in my best interest to leave my quote. I succumbed and watched her place it with the stack of other bids on the credenza behind her desk.

We got back in the car and that sinking feeling took over. It's a strange thing about the sales profession. A lot of salespeople work invisibly. They work alone and rarely does any manager see salespeople doing their actual job with a customer. Abe wasn't like that. He made sure he inspected the performance of his salespeople. Unlike most managers, he didn't take over and run the meetings. He didn't sit in his office demanding results either. He didn't yell. He went into the battle with you, observed, and helped. If he hadn't been on that sales call, nobody would have seen how poorly things had went and that hours of my work were reduced and compared to a pile of random numbers in a stack of papers on a credenza at an office with a person I never even met.

I was embarrassed because everything Abe said was true.

A few days later I would be told my price was too high. I didn't even know what Gary looked like or how many other companies bid for his work. I didn't know who had been supplying him products. I didn't know the first thing about his business. I didn't know a lot, except that one of Abe's lessons was coming…fortunately.

A few days later, after hearing I lost the sale, Abe walked into the bullpen and asked, "Want to avoid that situation in the future?"

"Yes," I said. Abe suggested I take some notes. That was when he introduced his "patented" move. He could see I was disappointed and embarrassed about the lost sale but refrained from criticizing me. He uses moments like these as opportunities to deliver advice when it is obviously needed. A warm feeling of comfort washed over me. In the past, he was fond of saying, "The teacher appears when the student is ready." It was more like the learning lesson always seemed to appear at the right time with him. I got my pen ready.

"Here is the situation," he said. "A buyer calls you. Maybe you call the buyer. Either way, you haven't interviewed them about their business challenges or buying practices. They tell you to give them a price and, *if* you're competitive, *then* they will talk to you. You suggest a meeting and they tell you to give a price first. Sound familiar?"

I nodded.

"Good," he said happily. "Here is the problem. You really can't bid properly because you don't know enough. The worst outcome might be that you actually get the business. If that happens based on nothing more than a price, a lot of red flags should go off in your mind, right?"

"I guess so," I said. I wasn't sure what red flags he meant, and Abe could tell.

"You might first wonder if you made a mistake and left some materials off your bid," he said. As soon as he said those words, I agreed that was a possible outcome. "You might get the business but lose it later in exactly the same way you gained it, by lowballing, when another competitor comes and lowballs *you* on a future project. You might get the sale and later discover it was easy because the buyer is a bad credit risk. You may discover that the buyer's service or delivery expectations were a lot more work than you anticipated and should have justified a higher price."

Abe looked down and, with a furrowed brow, said softly, as if he had just concluded an internal visionary dialogue with himself, "Yes. Lots can go wrong, even if you get the business in those situations."

He looked up at me. A smile returned to his face. "The next time someone asks you to provide a price without offering you an introductory dialogue, I want you to try something. Tell them you'll be too high."

Incredulously I asked, "Why would I tell a buyer that?"

Abe stated, "Because it's true! You should be high. You need to tell them they haven't shared their delivery or service expectations they will have *if* you get the business. Remember Image Builders. If you had known how much work was involved, you would have priced higher or perhaps even walked away. Additionally, you should know whether the opportunity is a one-time sale or the start of a long-term, high-volume relationship. You might be willing to price a little lower if you can sell a wider array of products. You might be able to sell a different product than the one requested if it potentially helps your buyer make more money. There is too much you don't know."

"So…I should tell a buyer all that instead of bidding?" I asked. As a young salesman just starting out, I found it hard to believe his method would work or that there was a way to convey that much information efficiently.

"Noah, you must," Abe said with paternal calmness. "It's in the buyer's best interest. Write this down. You tell them you need to know their service expectations, delivery expectations, expected volume, and other products you might add to the mix. You tell them you need to meet *before* pricing."

"And that really works?" I asked after finishing my notes.

Abe smiled and said, "Only 100% of the time."

"You get the meeting every time?" I asked skeptically.

Abe corrected me. "I didn't say that. I said it works every time…for a different reason. You might get the appointment, or you might not. If you get it, ring the bell. It's a victory. It's one step on the road to a new business relationship. On the other hand, the buyer might simply tell you, 'Nice try. I don't have time to meet. Bid or don't bid. Your choice. I don't care. I'm busy.'

"If a buyer said that to you, what would it tell you?" Abe asked.

"I'd guess they wouldn't be a very serious buyer."

"I agree!" Abe said enthusiastically. "But guess what! You can still price if you want to, but at least you tried to get the meeting. So, you lost nothing while still taking your best shot at a first meeting. You made the right *move*. You either get the appointment or you get good information. Therefore, it works every time. It's at least worth trying the move to get the appointment, yes?"

I nodded and smiled. The *bid avoidance* presentation was a solution to my problems. I immediately started using the technique and found out that a lot of buyers agreed to meet. I decided that the ones who refused might not be good prospects, thus I chose not to waste my time pricing their projects until we could meet.

I had always been a very energetic prospector. I made lots of calls and got many opportunities to bid until it reached a point at which I could hardly keep up. The bigger problem was that my closing ratios were lower than all the other salespeople. I realized it was because I was too anxious. I was bidding too much and not understanding situations properly.

"Do you golf?" Abe asked.

"I like to golf," I said. "Yes."

"Has anyone ever told you to grip the club as hard as you can and swing harder?"

I laughed and said, "No. Just the opposite. I've learned that you have to pace your swing and relax into it."

"Good," Abe said. "That's how selling is."

As John and I stare each other down for the first half-second of the negotiation, the memory of our first conversation at his jobsite enters my mind. I was lucky to catch him in the field on a cold call. He told me I could pick up a set of plans that day from the Mahogany Builders office. He said the windows had already been ordered for that job, but wanted a price to compare prices to his current supplier. In short, he was asking me to price a job I had no chance of getting. John said we'd sit down to meet after I put my pricing together.

You might think his request was surprising, but it isn't. Buyers ask for instant pricing in a variety of ways. Some have asked me to pick up an extensive list of materials they wanted me to price before they would meet. Others just e-mail the list as a "favor" to save me time. Some demand a generic price list from which they'd create their own competitive comparisons. They all ask to speed up the conversations and gain an upper hand in negotiations.

I didn't accept John's offer. "I'd rather bid on a future project instead," I said. "Even then, I would need to ask you some questions to be competitive." He asked me what I wanted to know, and I told him I needed to know his delivery and service expectations. I told him I would be able to price properly after I had a better sense of how much he builds. I asked if we could talk about those things.

After I delivered my "bid avoidance" speech John said, "This is not a good time. Here is my card. Give me a call tomorrow and we'll talk about what I'm looking for in a supplier."

I got in my car and felt strange pride. I took the first step toward a quality business relationship. If nothing else, I avoided a lot of work on a project I had no chance of getting. Instead, I teed up the opportunity for a very lucrative relationship.

"Speed is the enemy of profit," Abe always says.

In this case, I chalked up a victory for being slow and diligent. It was the right *move* in the situation.

6

You Choose Your Customers

"You can choose your customers, or they will choose you," Abe said.

Those words echoed momentarily while I tried to comprehend them. *You can choose your customers, or they will choose you.* "What does that mean?" I asked.

"It means finding good customers," Abe said. "It means avoiding problem ones before they become problems."

Abe walked to his white board, on which he had, by then, written in red letters, "Do Not Erase." The "dirty water" theory was an evolving concept for him. I felt lucky that I was the student with whom he was ferreting out his ideas. He erased the words *wrong buyers* and replaced them with **Prospecting Vision**.

BEAT THE PRICE OBJECTION

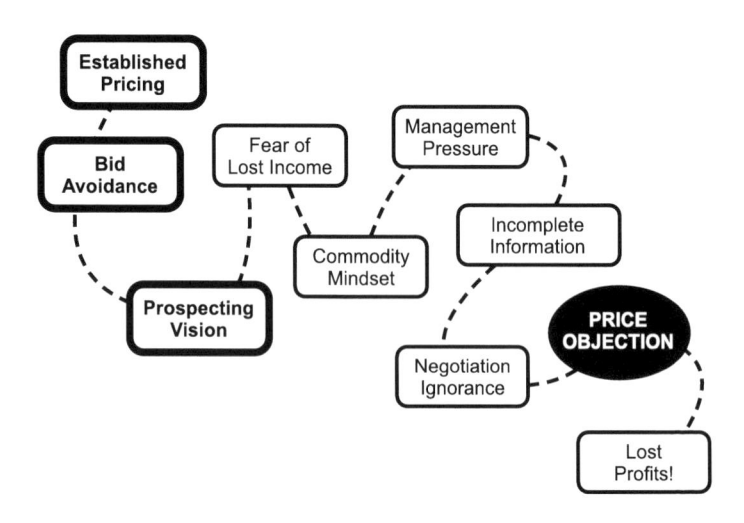

```
Established
  Pricing
     ↘
  Bid         Fear of      Management
Avoidance   Lost Income    Pressure
     ↘          ↓              ↘
                            Incomplete
                            Information
              Commodity         ↓
               Mindset
     ↗                        PRICE
Prospecting                 OBJECTION
  Vision
              Negotiation       ↓
              Ignorance
                              Lost
                             Profits!
```

He sat down and asked me, "What type of salesperson do the worst customers want?" I didn't know what he meant by the "worst customers," and he explained. "The worst customers are disloyal, constantly pressuring you for a lower price, always asking you to do more work, and sometimes very unfriendly. Ever met anyone like that?"

It made me think of a few customers I acquired during the previous months. I told Abe they were high nuisance headaches, and he agreed. "They are not the types of buyers you want, are they?"

"No," I admitted. "They're not, but what can I do?"

"My thought for you is to analyze *what type of salesperson those buyers are seeking*," Abe said, carefully enunciating his last words. "Think about it. If you were a really tough customer, what kind of salesperson would you want?"

I had never thought about his unique question. After considering it, I suggested, "They'd probably want a salesperson who is a bad negotiator. They'd want one who can be easily pushed around."

Abe waited for more. I recognized again that he wanted me to figure things out for myself. Thus, I pondered and said, "They probably want someone who knows a lot about products and does all the work for the buyer at a low price. That way they could dump more tasks on that salesperson and make them jump through hoops to earn the business."

Abe said, "I think you answered the question better than I could. Do you think you have any customers like that?"

"Yes. In fact, I think I'd like to get rid of them. Can a salesperson fire a customer?" I asked Abe.

"Of course, but it's a good idea to have some alternatives lined up." Abe chuckled and asked, "Got prospects?"

I laughed at his reference to the milk commercial tagline. Then, I thought about it and concluded. "I definitely have a lot of prospects, but how do I know which is a good alternative to my bad customers?"

"Perfect question!" Abe said with an eastern European accent while pointing his index finger into the air like a mad scientist once again. I laughed at his comical Sigmund Freud impersonation. Then he asked me, "If you paint the picture of the perfect customer, what would it look like?"

"The perfect customer?" I mused.

"Yep. The perfect one."

"I'm not sure the perfect one exists, does it?" I asked Abe.

"I think there are a lot out there if you go find them. But you have to first know what you're looking for. Can you tell me that?" Then he added, "If you can't envision it, you won't know it when you find it."

"I wish customers would respect my time," I said. Abe scribbled a few words on his notepad. I had to think about it for a little longer before adding, "I definitely want someone who is loyal."

"Great," Abe said. "Those are two good characteristics."

My mind was a blank until Abe prompted me. "What kind of volume are you looking for?" he asked.

"High volume!" I blurted proudly. I expected that to be an easy answer until Abe slowed me down.

"Would you rather have one $2,000,000 customer you rely on for all your business or ten $200,000 customers?" he asked.

I thought about that and cleverly said, "I want both! Can I have a $4,000,000 territory and have both?"

Abe, ever the sagacious leader, said, "You can for sure! I love the way you're thinking. But right now, you're at $1,000,000 with a bunch of customers you don't like so much. Let's get to $2,000,000 first and then worry about $4,000,000. How would you start?"

"I guess I'd start with that $2,000,000 account and then build from there?" I concluded.

"Great," Abe said. "Except, there aren't many of them out there. Besides, they take a long time to cultivate. Then they wield strong buying power and chew up your time, which in turn stifles your ability to find more business because you are so busy servicing the big account you cannot afford to lose. Ultimately, if you lose that single $2,000,000 account, where are you?"

"In big trouble and back to zero," I said before agreeing it would easier to find a group of mid-sized customers and build from there.

"Good thinking," Abe said. "But you can do what you want. My experience tells me that the best method of building your book of business is to find a large group of small to mid-sized accounts. Hunt deer and rabbit. They are more plentiful, easier to capture, and a lot less maintenance than the large elephant."

Abe told me I could "do what I want," but I knew better. His advice was solid. We continued to talk about the ideal customer. By the time we were done, he turned his pad to show me the list of criteria we created together.

> **The Ideal Customer**
> - ✔ Loyal
> - ✔ Cooperative Negotiator
> - ✔ Willing Planner
> - ✔ Target Volume
> - ✔ Long-Term Potential
> - ✔ Buys Standard Products
> - ✔ Low Nuisance Factor
> - ✔ Fair Margins
> - ✔ Pays Promptly

"Are there cooperative negotiators out there?" I asked, to which Abe pointed out several customers who negotiate very little with us and accept our pricing. He also noted they willingly invested time to get the right information into my hands. Some buyers are always rushed and don't give you the time you need to accurately get the job done. They expect you to figure it out. The ones that work with you he called "willing planners."

"What is the 'Low Nuisance Factor?'" I asked Abe.

"You said you want someone who respects your time, yes?" he asked, before adding, "How will you know if they do?"

I had to think about that and said, "There are things that a salesperson should do which are reasonable. Some customers are unreasonable, though."

"Exactly," said Abe. "There is a balance. Some customers make it worth going the extra mile. Some ask you to fly across the state and back, almost literally, to constantly put out their fires." He paused and asked, "Do you know what *integrity* means?"

"I think it means honest, right?"

Abe nodded. "It can," he said. "But integrity is something bigger. It means *alignment*. So, if you had a very loyal customer that paid fair profit margins, you'd probably be willing to do a little extra work for them, yes?"

"Of course." I nodded and listened for more.

"If you have a customer that always needs you to find special products instead of the standard products, it would be fair for them to pay a little extra to compensate for additional time you put in for them, yes?" he asked.

I agreed and asked, "Is that what you mean by 'buys standard products?'"

Abe smiled and said, "Exactly! It's more difficult to fulfill orders from people who want you to constantly find special materials. It's easier to manage customers that buy your standard products. And it's not just products. Some buyers are always asking for special delivery favors or trying to negotiate special terms. Every time someone wants a special service, it adds to your costs.

"Integrity means *alignment* between characteristics. It means you might not get a perfect match on all of the characteristics on our list, but that you're looking for alignment between them."

He sat back and asked, "Do you know where the term 'prospecting' comes from?" he asked.

"Yes. It's from the old days of prospecting for gold."

"Right," Abe said. Instead of giving the answer, he asked me one of those questions to which he already had the answer. "So how did they do that?"

"They sifted," I said. Abe nodded and waited for me to continue. "Well, that's it. They sifted." Abe kept silent until I said, "I guess they sifted and tossed out the dirt and rocks that were worthless and they saved the valuable nuggets for themselves."

"Perfect," said Abe. "That's it. You're searching for the right nugget. All the customers you have now that are pushing you around and negotiating combatively, they're not the ideal nuggets of gold. The dirty water at the mouth of the river is created by settling for the wrong buyers. The water gets cleaned upstream when you find the right ones.

"There are tangible benefits you seek such as volume and margins. There are intangible judgement calls you make about cooperation and willingness. You get a feel for buyers and whether or not they give you the information necessary to do the right job for them. Good buyers negotiate fairly and expect you to return the favor.

"Remember when I said the key to selling is locating the right customers. People too often believe selling is about persuasion, and that is *part* of it, but not as important as making the job easy by locating the right buyer. You sift to find the easy opportunities. Ever met anyone like that? Someone who was particularly easy to work with…?"

Without hesitation, I said, "Charley Moore."

Abe nodded and softly echoed Charley's name. "It seems like he's always being fair with me," I said. "That time we had a delivery glitch, he sent one of his guys to pick up materials. The time I left some materials off his delivery, he didn't yell, but just requested that the missing goods arrive the next day."

Charley Moore owns a small remodeling company that gives me about $15,000 per month in business. I said, "I'd like to have a few dozen of them. It's amazing, too, because everything was easy right from the start."

Abe grinned and asked, "Are you saying it was 'sale at first sight?'" Abe asked.

I laughed and said, "yes!"

"Good," said Abe. "That is sales vision. You know the right opportunity when you see it. How many of the people you've been pricing fall into the Charley Moore category?"

I pondered his question and admitted, "I really don't know because I haven't started doing business with most of them."

"That's the point," Abe said. "You're bidding before you even start the dialogue. You need to slow things down. Remember, speed is the enemy of profit. You've been asking for opportunities to bid instead of asking for opportunities to open a relationship.

"This is the power of *bid avoidance*. It enables you to have the dialogue which reveals the right opportunities. You know if the buyers have the characteristics you seek *before* you give them a price. You clean the dirty water upstream.

"Don't underestimate my comment about long-term potential," Abe added. "You have been working with a lot of homeowners because they walk in and are easy leads to acquire. They also require the most work because they are not well-versed in construction practices. They provide a one-time sale and leave you constantly having to find new buyers. You should see them as leads for your customers and prospects, the professionals who are experts at working with homeowners."

"Right now, you are letting buyers choose you for all the wrong reasons stated earlier. They'll buy from you if you're a low bidder and willing to jump through hoops. You're pricing the uncooperative, combative negotiators who seek *their* ideal salesperson willing to do all the work at a low price. It is the reason your closing ratios are low. You're willing to put in all the work they don't see. By the time you're done, your offer is simply a price, the only criterion they have to distinguish you from others."

The next day I tried Abe's "bid avoidance" move for the first time. I wasn't as smooth as Abe was, but clumsily explained that my price would be best if I knew more about their delivery and service requirements. I told them that the more volume they do, the lower my price can be and that we should meet first.

Two people I spoke with were unwilling to meet with me. One was rude and said, "you can price it or not. If you're competitive, then I'll have time for you." The other said he was "just too busy for another salesperson." A few days earlier, I probably would have engaged in the behavior Abe calls the "bid and pray" sales method. Instead, I continued sifting to find more suitable prospects.

The day after I met John at his jobsite, I called to schedule an appointment. Strangely his response came as if we had never met. Even though I had used the bid avoidance technique the day before and it seemingly worked, he put me to the test once again. He told me he needed to see some pricing to ensure I was competitive.

I used the bid avoidance technique with him a second time. My words were, "John, like I said at the jobsite yesterday, I can't be competitive without knowing more about your service and delivery expectations. Plus, I don't know if this is just a one-time deal or if you are interested in a relationship with a dependable supplier in the future. So.. um…"

John chimed in and said, "When were you thinking?"

"Meaning to meet and discuss your business?" I asked.

"I don't want to date you…so yes, let's discuss business. When?" John said. He was direct and, as I suddenly learned, had a dry sense of humor.

"Um…tomorrow?" I asked. He agreed and told me to be at his office at 8:00.

My heart lifted and my body relaxed. It worked. I had avoided wasting my time pricing blindly in another bidding war and scheduled the meeting with John Henderson.

7

Abundance Happens Between Your Ears

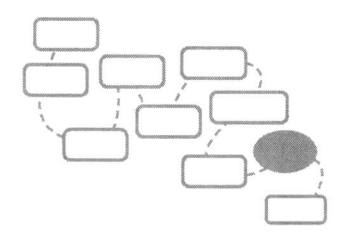

Abe joined me on the first sales meeting I had with John Henderson. I was intimidated by the quality of his home office and the type of houses he built. They are mansions. Mahogany Builder's clientele includes people famous enough that John won't divulge their names save for "a need-to-know basis."

As Abe observed the first meeting, I intently questioned John about the products he was purchasing; who he purchased those products from; what he liked about them; what he didn't like; and what we needed to do to earn his business. The meeting ended with John telling me he had a project he'd let me bid on in the coming weeks.

To end the meeting, I suggested that I at least bring in a window sample for John to see. He agreed it was a good idea and we set up a time to meet the following week.

We left and Abe asked me some questions. The first was, "Where does John get his leads?"

"You mean his sales leads?" I asked. Abe nodded.

"Um…I dunno," I said with a shrug. I couldn't see how it mattered to the sale.

Abe asked, "How did he start his business?" I drove and wondered where Abe's questions were leading. I admitted I had no idea how John started his business.

Abe fired a number of questions my way. "What do you think his biggest challenges are when he is building houses or doing remodeling projects? I wonder how he manages people, don't you? How many people do you figure he has working for him?" Abe wasn't really rude when he asked me these questions. It was more like he was thinking out loud. Finally, he said, "What do you think?"

"About what?" I asked as my eyes focused on the road toward our next meeting.

"All those things I just mentioned," Abe said, as if they were mere curiosities rather than important business issues.

"I guess those are pretty good things to know," I admitted. I was feeling embarrassed because Abe was trying to make a point and I was missing it.

He let the silence linger and finally said, "So, if we give him a price, I wonder how he gets one of his buyers to agree to accept our windows." He waited before adding matter-of-factly, "Do you suppose someone building a large mansion overlooking Lake Michigan just accepts the product decisions of the builder or would they be involved in the window selection?"

It hit me finally. Abe's questions made me realize the things I didn't know about John Henderson and Mahogany Builders were a lot! The product decisions John makes would, of course, involve his customers. I realized that John doesn't just build houses. He has buyers to appease and deadlines to meet. I realized that he had customers who were probably very demanding.

Abe calmly asked, "What do you think people like to talk about most?"

I smiled and acknowledged, "Themselves."

Abe nodded and it felt good to get one of his questions right. He said, "You asked a lot of questions and shared a lot of information about products. Who were you talking about?"

"Us," I admitted with some embarrassment.

Abe said, "Do you want to know what you did extremely well?"

Abe waited. I drove. I thought it was a rhetorical question and realized he wanted an answer. I finally said, "Yes!"

"You scheduled a meeting with him to show a window sample next week. That's the sales secret we spoke of early in your training. You got the next meeting. As long as you keep doing that to create sales momentum, you'll do well."

Abe provided insights into his coaching. He explained why he resists interjecting during sales calls. "It sets a bad tone and indicates lack of confidence in the salesperson. Besides," he added, "most of the time I won't be there to help. How can I help you perform better when I'm not looking if I don't pay attention when I am looking? A good coach first observes before teaching or demonstrating. If I jump into the conversation, recognize it is to illustrate a skill you can learn. I'm not selling for you. I'm showing you how to do it without me. Do you understand?"

I nodded and kept driving. Being with Abe was intense, but a great experience if you can stick with him. He continued, "I would have jumped into the conversation to ask questions and demonstrate some listening skills with John. But, after you scheduled that next meeting, I figured we had time to work on your listening skills. What do you think about that idea?"

I loved the idea and told Abe so before adding, "I'd like to find about a dozen customers like John."

Abe said, "Funny you should mention that. I was about to suggest you find a few dozen *prospects* like John, and maybe some who are not, yet still equally valuable because they build different types of homes."

I hesitated to respond, figuring there was more to Abe's logic. I was right. He added, "First, you might discover that it takes three or four prospects to get one customer. That's how selling works. It's a percentage game, right?"

"You're saying that I'll need 48 prospects to get 12 customers?"

"Yes. Maybe." Abe said. "Maybe you'll need 75 prospects. Maybe 25. It depends on your closing ratios."

Abe continued, "The thing I want you to think about now is how to get someone to buy at your telling price. The more prospects you have, the more confidence you'll have in holding your price. In the coming weeks, you will be giving John a price, yes?"

I agreed.

"What if he tells you your price is too high? Then what?"

I thought about it. I already felt the fear salespeople get about losing a sale, even before giving their price. So, I confessed, "Well, I'll be nervous that we're too high. If he says I am, my gut reaction would be to ask where I need to be."

Abe said, "I have an idea that could work if you want it."

Abe waited and let the silence linger until I finally said, "Yes. What's the idea?"

Abe got serious and I knew a good tip was coming "You meet with John and his staff a few times. You listen to carefully understand his business. You invest hours driving, listening, pricing, and writing up a proposal. Then, after all the hours, days, and weeks of energy you've invested, just deliver a proposal to John, and tell him, 'You just fill in the price there in the blank and let me know where I need to be. Because I really don't have a clue.'"

I was stunned before I noticed Abe beaming with a huge smile.

Finally, I laughed as much out of embarrassment as the comedy of his statement. Abe said, "Isn't that what a salesperson is doing when they ask, 'where they need to be?'" He didn't expect an answer before continuing, "Or, on the other hand…

"Let's say you slow down and do the best job of establishing value with each prospect. Let's say you work to find a whole bunch of prospects so that one or two rejections doesn't feel so badly because you have a lot more opportunities in your pipeline. While we're at it," Abe said, continuing his stream of consciousness, "Let's say first we discover more about our buyers' businesses to determine how we can help them succeed. That way you might improve your percentages, don't you think?"

I nodded.

"Then," Abe continued, "we'll gauge how they fit into our criteria of the perfect customer. After that, you'll price them accordingly. Does that make sense?"

It did. Abe made me feel a lot more comfortable about the process. Then he asked again what I would do if John pressured for a lower price.

I thought carefully and responded truthfully. "I'd like to hold it firm," I said. "Truthfully, I don't know if I'd have the courage. I feel I need the business."

"Great answer," Abe said, which surprised me. "Why?"

"Why what?" I asked.

"Why do you feel you need John's business?"

I thought about it and said what any other salesperson might say, "I need to grow my sales."

Abe said, "There's more. The problem is that you don't have enough high-quality prospects. The opportunity with John is very valuable, but the fear of losing it is magnified because and you don't have comparable alternatives readily available. However, if you had a half dozen more sales leads like this one, you could trust that you might not get all of them, but at least you'll get one or two. Does that make sense?"

"Well, I'd like to get them all," I proudly stated, realizing my declaration sounded like the false bravado of most young salespeople. Abe said it was great that I feel deserving of getting every sale I shoot for. He then asked if I should get it by lowering our margins or if I should get it at my telling price.

"I'd like to get it at my telling price," I told him. I was paid based on profits and therefore wanted to keep them high. That was my incentive.

"Let's just figure you want them all, but for now presume some will accept your telling price while others aren't going to be seriously interested and let you price anyway. This is why you practice bid avoidance. Finally, a lot are going to ask you to negotiate. The simple question is this: do you feel more confident holding your price when you have alternative options available?"

I said, "I definitely would be more confident walking away from a negotiation if I knew I had alternative options in my sales pipeline."

Abe said nothing more while I continued driving in the I-94 congestion of Chicago as my mind became equally congested. I found someone who actually gave me time and quality dialogue and was overly excited about getting the business. If I could find more prospects just like Mahogany Builders, I'd be in a better position to hold my price. If not, I'll feel like the lone sales opportunity is an all-or-nothing proposition.

We got to the office and another salesman, Adam, was in the bullpen doing paperwork. He also had been privy to Abe's "dirty water" theory on the price objection. Abe walked to his white board and erased *fear of lost income*.

He said, "We fear a lost sale because our mind perceives opportunities for success are scarce. We limit our thinking and end up operating from a perspective of fear. Abundance, however, gives you confidence. It enables you to reduce or eliminate the fear of a lost sale because you have alternatives in your prospecting pipeline.

"The mistake most salespeople make is to believe that abundance is an economic market condition. It's not," Abe said before concluding, "Abundance happens between your own two ears. You create your own perception of abundance."

Adam looked up and listened. He had experienced the lessons of Abe Isaacson and knew when a valuable new one was on the way. Abe continued, "The mistake we salespeople make is that we are eager to take credit for sales growth when business is booming. We don't like to take the blame when it's not. The problem is that all ships rise and dip with the tide.

"The market fluctuates. It also rises and falls like the tides. Good salesmanship, however, is steady. It is not dependent on the abundance or scarcity of economic tides. Success in sales means rising above them, not just in volume, but profit. Successful sales leaders create abundance by prospecting at all times."

He wrote new words inside the box and made the border bolder. "Gentlemen," he said. "Let's replace the fear of lost income with *Prospecting Abundance*. What do you think that does for you in the heat of a negotiation battle?"

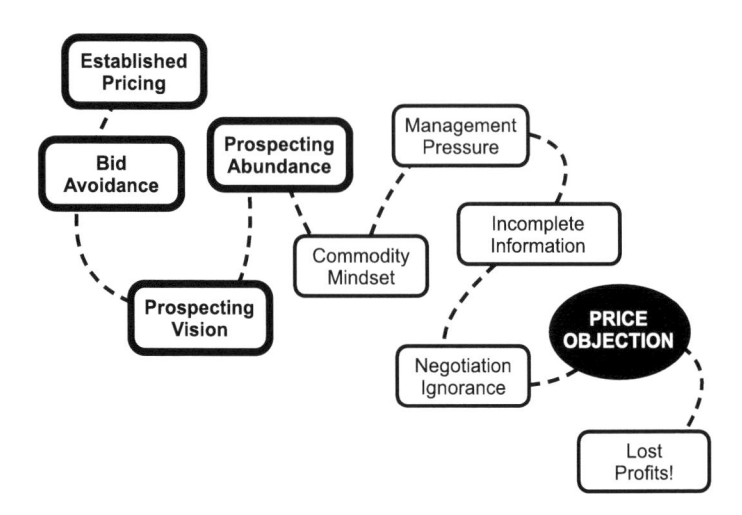

Abundance Happens Between Your Ears

Adam smiled because Abe had already taught him the value of prospecting energy. "You know it's helped me," he said to Abe. Then Adam turned to me and said, "Let's say your *only* prospect is John Doe Builder and you decide to hold your price. You're pretty scared because, if you lose the sale, you have nothing."

I nodded.

Adam continued, "And really…if you do hold your price, it *actually* is a risk, except that John Doe doesn't know it. The reason you feel pressure is not John Doe. It's you!"

I contemplated his words and nodded again.

"It's a bad feeling," Adam said, "and you experience deep fear because you have no other options, right?"

Adam continued like a mini-Abe. I could tell he had been through Abe's process and became a staunch advocate. "Now let's say you have lots of prospects and John Doe Builder is only one of the many. You confidently hold your price because you have alternatives. The situation is the same to John Doe, but you're in a better negotiation position and feeling confident even if you lose the sale. Same situation, but very different perspective."

Abe chimed in, "I don't think I could have explained it any better. Think about what Adam just said…

"The market doesn't change. The power you have to change the so-called market conditions is based solely on the abundance you create, not the market itself. It's perception. For the buyer, you are nothing more than a potential supplier in a one-on-one dialogue. The buyer is counting on you negotiating from a perspective of scarcity. However, it is not one-on-one to you when you create abundance; the opportunity becomes one-of-many. That's sales power."

Abe smiled and turned to Adam, "Although, I have one question? Are you saying you feel no anxiety when you hold your price even when you have other prospects in your pipeline?"

Adam thoughtfully paused and said, "Um, no. I still shake in my boots…but now the buyer can't tell!"

We all had a laugh and Abe said, "I don't think the anxiety ever goes away, but it sure gets easier when you have a lot of other customers and prospects to choose from."

"The truth is," Adam said to me, "it's more than prospecting. If you are building a good network of customers, not just prospects, it helps. The important thing is that the negotiation is different when you're negotiating from a perspective of confidence."

Abe said, "Noah, the point Adam is conveying is that you can wait until you have that book of business to give you confidence or you can prospect to build the confidence. Either way, you create your own perspective and power by cultivating alternative choices. Power is choice.

"We have a saying around here," Abe said. "Dance like nobody is watching. Sing like nobody is listening…"

Adam chimed in for the last words of the saying and echoed with Abe, "Sell like you don't need it." They both laughed.

Abe was still smiling as he walked toward the door before turning to ask me, "Mind if I tag along for your next meeting with John? I might be able to help."

"Do I have a choice?" I asked, realizing instantly I sounded like a smart aleck in front of these intelligent sales leaders.

Adam chimed in, "Of course you do, but the wise move is to take the help."

Abe agreed, "It's an offer. You do have a choice."

Adam was obviously right. Abe could help and the smart move was to accept his guidance. I said, "I'll take it."

The lesson was learned. The price objection is truly like dirty water at the mouth of the river. If you don't have ample alternatives *prior* to a negotiation, your leverage is weakened *during* the negotiation. The buyer might not know anything about the other work I'm doing upstream, but it has an effect on the power dynamic. Knowing I have alternatives might not take the sting out of losing a sale, but it certainly makes me a confident negotiator because I can remain optimistic about other opportunities.

As Abe said, the tension never goes away, and the anxiety I feel is very real while sitting in front of John Henderson. He presents the exact type of opportunity I would hate to lose. However, the only way I will ever learn if he pays fair margins is to test the waters and hold firm.

Logic reminds me this is *not* an all-or-nothing sales moment. It dawns on me that I'm actually getting busy with a lot of new clients. If I'm going to take on another one, it has to be worth my time. I've built up a list of credible prospects too. The messages from the logical portion of my brain, however, are in combat with the fight or flight impulses from my primitive medulla oblongata.

The sales devil and sales angel are standing on my shoulders going to war, each spouting ideas into my ears. The sales devil whispers, "Take the deal, moron. You get a commission no matter what the margin." He's right! Logic and sensibility be damned. I want the sale! Why not cave a little and ensure that my new client is happy? My job is to put food on the table.

The sales devil tells me to lower my price on the first transaction with Mahogany Builders. He says I can inch up my profits later, but an earlier lesson from Abe rings in my ear. "It's a risk," he told me. "If you lowball a price to earn business and later raise your prices, you often find you lose your credibility and business to the next lowball price. It's not the way to establish trust or profits."

The sales angel is advising me in my other ear to do the right thing for my customer, Acme windows. The sales devil's push to act purely in my own self-interest is diminished when I think about my reputation with Abe. I consider that John might not hold me in high regard either. Then again, I think about what I could buy with additional income. On the other hand, I think about the many implications of lowering my price. The devil and angel are now screaming, and both are starting to irritate me.

Their voices are so loud that I suspect John can hear them. It's a split second in time since he told me I need to do a "little better" while the lessons of Abe flash in my brain. My heart is pulsing faster and there is no time to lose. The iconic image of *the scream* painted by Edvard Munch flashes before me.

8

People Care How Much You Care

Prior to my second meeting with John, I spent the week prospecting for new sales opportunities. I knew Abe expected our time on the road to be more productive than a single meeting with one prospect. He calls it *game day* and gets excited about seeing how well a salesperson can fill a day with productive meetings.

A lot of buyers told me they wanted a price from me but didn't have time to meet. Naturally, I avoided them. I got through on two phone calls and scheduled appointments. Some companies had people answering the phone who made it difficult to get to the decision maker.

Adam was in the bullpen and could hear me on the phone. He heard people hanging up on me and sensed my frustration. I got a bit rude and realized it was not going to help my efforts. It was embarrassing and became worse when Adam started laughing.

"What so funny?" I asked defensively.

He said, "I was thinking about the time Abe walked in on me as I was yelling at someone on the phone while doing the exact thing you're doing today. It was my *first* day on the job and about the most embarrassing moment I've ever had working here."

I felt Adam's pain because I knew how much I wanted to avoid disappointing Abe. "Did he lose it?" I asked Adam.

Adam smiled and said, "You're just getting to know Abe. I've seen him get tough on salespeople, but they deserved it. The ones who keep trying get a lot of latitude."

"So…he didn't lose it?" I asked.

"No," Adam said. "He didn't lose it. Not at all. He was way cool. In fact, he sat down and started making phone calls with me. He set up appointments."

My raised eyebrows stated my surprise. "Does that really surprise you, Noah?" Adam asked. I thought about it and figured it shouldn't. Abe wasn't like most sales managers who might not have the ability to demonstrate a cold call and, therefore, fear the failure of being exposed. He didn't sit back and tell you to do things he couldn't do. He was willing to demonstrate. Adam then asked me if I wanted a tip.

"Anything that will help," I said.

"Make it more conversational. You're using all the phrases Abe taught me that work. One thing you're doing wrong is trying to speak with just one person. Get to know everyone."

"What do you mean," I asked.

Adam said, "Start by getting the name of the person you're talking to. Then, instead of asking 'Who is the person making decisions,' change your question to, 'Would you mind helping me by sharing the name of the person I should talk with?'"

I asked him to repeat that phrase and decided I would use it. It worked immediately! The only problem was that the person wasn't in. Adam pretended he wasn't listening, but I knew he was. I picked up the phone to make the next call and Adam interrupted, "Who was the person you were supposed to speak with?"

I wasn't ready for his question and had to think about it before saying, "'She said… um… Harry.' That's his name. He is the man in charge."

Adam nodded. He was like an Abe impersonator in some ways. "If you struggle to remember it one minute after the call, how likely are you to remember it when you call back in a few days?"

I nodded and wrote Harry's name on a piece of paper next to his company name. Then Adam asked me who I spoke with to get Harry's name. I blushed because I had no idea and hadn't asked who I was speaking to.

A moment later, Adam heard me say, "Hi. I'm Noah from Acme Windows."

"Hi, Elizabeth," he heard me say after a pause. He also saw me write her name as I said, "I've seen your company's signs on job sites and thought we might be a good fit for your company. Would you be willing to help me out and tell me the best person to speak with?"

"Great!" I responded. "Is Mike Lewis in?"

Mike wasn't. Elizabeth asked me for my information and suggested I call back later in the week. Adam pretended he wasn't listening. Then he packed up his papers to head for an appointment.

He turned at the door and said, "You're going to be fine. Trust the process. The little things add up to big success."

I spent the remainder of the week looking for good contacts to meet. I lined up numerous quality meetings with prospects and they were all solid companies to work with. During that week, Abe set up his schedule so he could invest time with me at various sales calls, including my second meeting with John Henderson.

Prior to entering John's office, Abe asked if he could lead the meeting and, naturally, I agreed. I wanted to see him in action. We shook hands with John and sat across his desk. Abe waited for me to set the window sample in the corner and then ignored it.

"John, we have a sample for you but, if you don't mind, please tell us a bit about your business first," Abe said.

"What do you want to know?"

I confess that, had Abe been absent, no questions would have come to mind except to ask who he buys windows from. I hadn't progressed beyond that.

"Tell us how you built your business or how you go to market or where you get your leads," Abe said. He was sitting calmly with his legs crossed. He extended an open palm as a gesture to say in the friendliest way, without words, "We're an open book, Sir. You have the floor."

John explained that his father was a builder, and he learned the trade from him. He said that his father was passionate about John getting a college degree, which he did from the University of Illinois. He studied business and majored in marketing, "which has helped me a lot," he said.

Abe sat calmly when there was, for me, an uncomfortable moment of silence. I felt one of us should say something but decided he knew what he was doing.

"We get good word of mouth," John said, picking up steam again. "We try to get about four to five new projects per year. They're big," he said with a gleam in his eye. He was proud of the type of houses he built. He stated that his networking group included members of his golf club, relationships with several architects on Chicago's north shore, and referrals. "We keep pretty busy," he concluded proudly.

"And how do you run this well-oiled machine?" Abe asked. His question was amazing in its simplicity and direction while being complimentary at the same time.

John didn't hesitate to proudly describe his team of amazing subcontractors. He had two framing companies he worked with and a network of tradespeople. He smiled and added, "Jimmy runs the projects." He looked toward me and said, "He couldn't be here today, but you should meet him. He's at one of our projects today, not far from here." John shared more while I took notes.

He looked back at Abe and said, "Tommy is my millwork guy. He works for me full time. He's the best. He's a prima donna, demanding, and the most difficult guy I've ever worked with," he said before adding with a wink, "Don't tick him off! I can't afford to lose him."

Abe and I smiled. By the time we left John's office, I had learned more about successful entrepreneurship and listening skills in the few minutes of Abe's questioning than my first three years of selling combined. I understood that John managed subcontractors, networked to get business, had scheduling challenges to address, and more.

Abe let me present our Prestige window model to John before we left his office. Even though Abe had expected me to create a full day of appointments, John was my third and last of the day. I hated to admit that to Abe because he taught me the power of appointments and calendar management.

"That's fortunate," he said. "Want to swing by that jobsite to meet Jimmy?"

I eagerly agreed it would be a good stop. On the way, Abe asked me to comment on his listening process.

"You mean like how you ask questions?"

"Well," Abe said as he leaned back comfortably in the passenger seat of my SUV. "It's not really about the questions. In fact, I think I only asked John three or four of them."

I replayed the conversation and agreed. I told Abe it was very cool to see him getting John to do all the talking. "There is an old saying," Abe told me. "People don't care how much you know until they know how much you care."

He continued, "Notice that I asked him to share a bit about his business. I like to know what the buyer values more, the operations side of business or marketing and sales. It's a business-focused question, but vague enough to let him tell us what he values most.

"We got a lot of information. He's well networked. People

know him and his business seems to be on solid footing. If you get his business, there is a good chance he'll introduce you to the architects he knows, but that wasn't the purpose of the question; it's a beneficial byproduct.

"I'd still like to understand his sales process," Abe added thoughtfully, "but that can be a conversation for another time. We found out a lot about his operational mindset. The fact that he employs a fussy, detail-oriented finish carpenter tells you about his attention to detail for his customers, which a high-end clientele probably expects, right?"

I nodded and volunteered, "It was amazing how much you got him to say."

Abe waved his hand as if it were nothing and said, "Everyone wants to tell their story, especially when it's such a good one like John's. Most salespeople don't take enough time to intentionally listen."

We pulled up to the job site and Abe told me to take the lead. I was nervous to have Abe quietly watching me. We moseyed up to a worker and asked to speak with Jimmy.

"You got him," he said. Jimmy was covered in sawdust and had a work belt with tools hanging from his waist. "Give me a minute." He was fit, short, with dark hair and friendly blue eyes. He spoke with a distinctive Irish lilt he undoubtedly brought off the boat a few years back. He called out to one of his workers, reminding him to plumb one of the interior door openings before coming back to Abe and me.

"What can I do ya for?" he asked. I asked if he came from Ireland. He smiled and said, "County Cork."

"I've been there," I said. Abe looked and I wondered if maybe the conversation was starting wrong, but he let me keep going. I decided to stop the small talk. "We just came from John Henderson's office. He told me it would be okay to introduce myself to you and drop my card."

Jimmy took the card and said, "Nice to meet you, Noah. And you are?"

"Abe." Abe extended his hand to shake and added, "I work with Noah and he's letting me tag along today to see if I can learn anything."

Jimmy probably knew the real role Abe played. He smiled and played along before asking, "Acme Windows, huh?"

"Yup," I said. "John has a project coming up that he thought we might be good for."

Jimmy volunteered a lot in that moment. "Probably because the goofballs at Pinnacle have dropped the ball so much," he said. "We've had some delays and, to tell the truth, I think it's just an okay window. Our customers don't seem to demand it, so John's probably shopping. Give him a price with a sharp pencil and you'll be in the runnin'."

We got back in the car and Abe smiled. "Congratulations. I'd say that's a good couple of sales calls. What do you think you need to do to earn this business?"

"I guess give him a sharp pencil and I'll be in the runnin,'" I said while imitating my best Irish brogue.

Abe smiled but didn't allow himself to be dissuaded from the bigger issue at hand. "Then you're missing it," he said. "He's setting you up for a price objection. That's what builders do. He's telling you to be the lowest price. He already throwing some dirt in the water upstream. You have to determine what is really going on here and clean up the mess before it's too late."

I was embarrassed because Abe makes it fun while, at the same time, it is easy to forget his intensity. I thought about the situation and said, "Well, I know we better get the goods there on time. That's obviously a problem."

Abe agreed and said, "That's it. Pinnacle has dropped the ball. He isn't going to tell you all the problems to make it easy for you, but you might be able to find out by driving by the jobsite a few times. That house is framed with no windows installed yet. Maybe they're delayed. In fact, they probably are. It's probably the reason we have this opportunity in the first place." Abe paused and asked, "When does a builder change to a new supplier?"

I thought about it for a moment and stated, more as a question than a sentence, "When they have problems with the existing one?"

"Yes. That's it. You showed up at the right time. You might have to wait for the right opportunity with other builders. In this case the timing is right, or lucky. There was something else, too. Jimmy said something else that gives you an opportunity. What was it?"

I racked my brain. If you, the reader, heard it, I'd like to know because I completely missed whatever it is that Abe was searching for.

"He said their customers don't seem to care much for Pinnacle, right?"

"Oh yeah," I said. "He did say that."

Abe said, "You might try, if you can, to get a meeting with the owners on a future project to let them see our product and, working with John, select the options they most would value. It's too late to get involved on their current project, but you can leverage the knowledge of the current situation to get the next one."

We drove silently the last few minutes back to the office. Abe shook my hand and looked me in the eye. He said, "Congratulations. You just surpassed *commodity credibility*. You're not going to price blindly. You're going to figure out how to become part of John's machine."

John stares at me waiting for my reaction to his negotiation pressure. I am thinking of the moment, one day after that meeting at the jobsite with Jimmy, when I saw Abe's evolving drawing. Commodity credibility had been replaced with the words **Consultative Credibility**. The positive voice negotiating for me in my head says, like the old self-help guru on Saturday Night Live, "Doggone it, Noah. You've earned this. You're good enough."

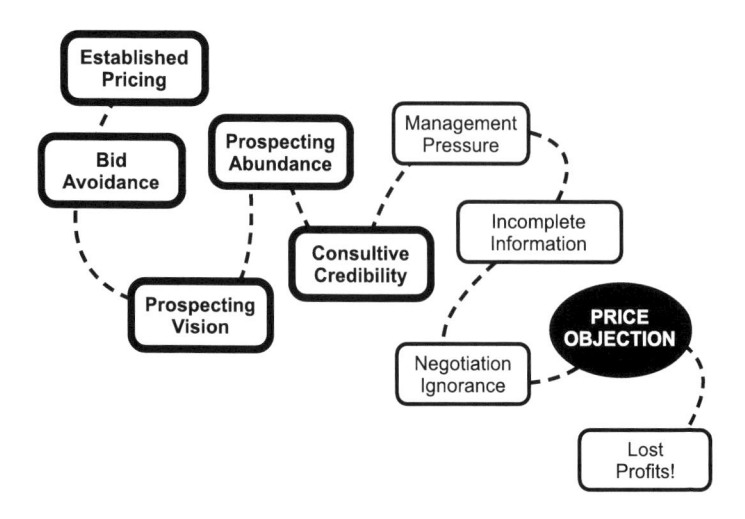

In the many weeks since I met Jimmy on the jobsite, a lot of things have happened. John has brought his client, the homeowner, to our showroom where we walked through the various options. Besides all the legwork I have put in to produce a high-quality, accurate proposal, I introduced a lumber sales representative who provided a level of detail and support that impressed John greatly. The lumber salesman has already taken the order for the lumber, the first portion of which is about to be delivered.

If I had bid based only on a quick look at a set of blueprints, I would have been nothing more than a salesperson pushing a commodity, no different than my competition. Instead, I had taken great pains to ensure accuracy of every product detail. I had clarified and made the right plans to have products available the day he needs them on the job. I had met with Jimmy and his crew to verify the proper construction details while delivering the window dimensions. In other words, I have provided a lot of consultive value. My price is a lot more than a random bid; it is an offer to get the job done right the first time.

Abe words rang in my ear, "People don't care how much you know until they know how much you care." I feel like I've given John a lot of my time and energy to help him succeed. I've proven to him how much I care about helping him. I think he should recognize it.

9

You Can't Measure What You Can't See

The pressure to produce results in sales is relentless. Last year's success is replaced by the pressure to do it again, only get more. The current sale is preceded by the pressure to get one more…and then another. Abe once told me selling is the "profession of fear." He said it violates every law of spirituality because it constantly pressures the salesperson to achieve *more*. He showed me and other salespeople how to overcome the fear by shifting the focus away from the outcome to the process under our control.

The morning before I had my fifth meeting with John Henderson, Abe walked into the bullpen where I had the blueprints for Mahogany Builders. Adam happened to be in the conference room at the same time, working on a blueprint, as we watched Abe walk to his whiteboard and erase the words *management pressure* from his diagram.

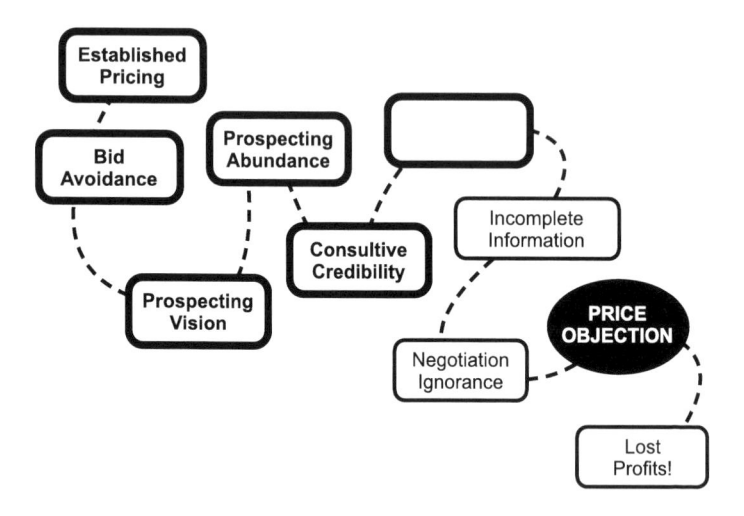

```
    Established
     Pricing
        |
    Bid          Prospecting
  Avoidance      Abundance         [ ]
        \           |              /
         \          |     Incomplete
          \    Consultive  Information
           \   Credibility        \
         Prospecting                 PRICE
           Vision                  OBJECTION
                  \                    \
                   Negotiation           \
                   Ignorance              Lost
                                         Profits!
```

"It's the pipeline that matters," he said to Adam and me. He smiled. "I have to admit that my thoughts before were incomplete. I've told both of you that the fear goes away when you focus on the process instead of the outcome, but that's only for the short term. Right?"

Ironically, we were both striving to close a couple of big deals at the time and Abe asked, "So do either of you feel completely relieved of the anxiety to get results. Has your focus on the sales process eliminated it?"

Adam looked at me and we both shrugged, unsure of our thoughts on the subject. Abe waited for an answer. Adam finally said, "I feel pretty confident about the process now that

I know *The Sales Secret* to closing a sale, but I guess there still is that anxiety any salesperson feels when worrying about long-term sales goals."

Abe looked at me and waited until I said, "My sales are the lowest in the company, but I guess I'm not as nervous as I used to be. In fact, I feel like good things are happening. I'm confident."

"Excellent! Why is that?" Abe knew the answer but wanted to see if I could figure it out also.

Adam grinned and asked, "Yeah wise guy, why is that?" He had started out where I was and became one of our top salespeople. Like Abe, he had a knack for making the learning fun and taking away some of the pressure I felt around our mentor.

I thought about it for a moment and finally said, "The data."

Abe smiled and Adam waited. Finally, Adam said, "That's it? The data?"

I saw Abe grinning and knew it was the right answer. "Yep," I said. "It's the data. A couple months ago I was bidding like crazy. My quote log was full of bad leads. Today, I have a prospecting pipeline with eight leads for the month, plus I know how to get more. I won't sell them all, but I'll get some."

Adam looked at me and smiled. He could see the evolution taking place in me. Abe also smiled and silently went to his drawing to write two new words.

He wrote **Performance Metrics**. He said to both of us, "The prospecting lists are for you, not me. My job is to help you keep them up to date to build your confidence, not to appease me. That's how you build career security.

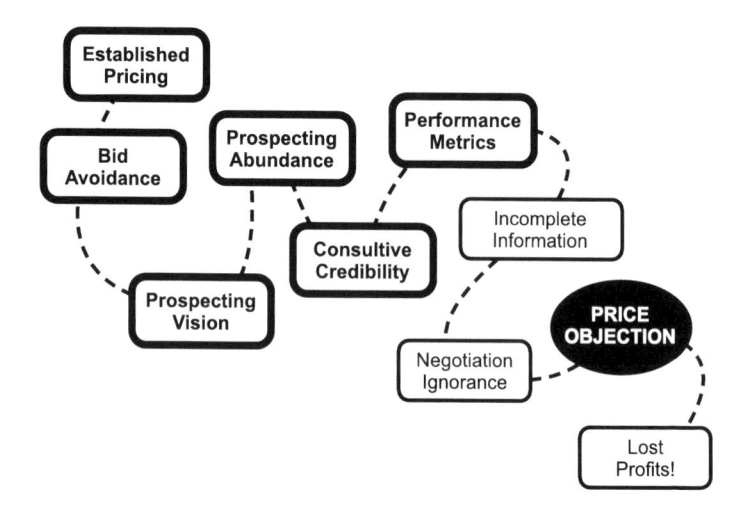

[Diagram: Established Pricing → Bid Avoidance; Prospecting Abundance; Performance Metrics; Consultive Credibility; Incomplete Information; Prospecting Vision; Negotiation Ignorance → **PRICE OBJECTION** → Lost Profits!]

"It's like two ends of a knife. If you grab it by the blade, it's a weapon; if you wield it by the handle, it's a tool. If I tell you to do this because I am watching, the metrics are a weapon for control. If I show you how they can help you succeed for the rest of your career, then they are a tool.

"It's also vital to beating the price objection. If you simply *think* you have enough in your pipeline, it's an illusion of hope. If you *know* the value and where your leads are coming from, then you know your future. You know if you can afford to lose a sale because the quantity of alternatives is as clear in your mind as it is on paper. Everyone knows you can't manage what you don't measure. But you can't measure what you can't see. You need documentation.

"Remember when I told you that Acme is our customer, Noah?"

I nodded.

"This is the service we provide. It's the service you both

provide. We let our customer, Acme, know we're giving them the best service possible with evidence of our work. Documentation. We're uncovering opportunities in the market. We're bringing in the right kind of business. We do it by canvasing the market and selecting the right accounts. The information we provide to ourselves is the data we provide our customer, Acme, as evidence of the work we are accomplishing.

"We *choose* the right customers for Acme."

"You told me earlier about knowing what we *want* in an ideal buyer, but how do we get to choose?" I asked.

Abe said. "Remember the criteria we're seeking in an ideal customer, yes?"

Adam watched and I nodded.

He said, "We know the parameters of a good buyer, and they know what they want in a supplier. We sell the products we can provide easily in the time frame to which we can commit at a fair price. If the buyer wants something we can't easily provide or wants to buy it at a price that is not profitable, we choose to find a different buyer. If we find a buyer that fits the integrity and alignment of the right criteria, then we know we've chosen the right one…and they have chosen well too!"

"The price determines our choice by establishing the value we place on the buyer's business as well as the cost of doing business. We deliver the appropriate telling price and expect them to pay it. We don't reject a prospect because we don't like them or deem them unworthy of our time. Instead, we know the right price for the level of service requested. In a way, we choose each other."

Adam piped in, "That makes total sense. That's what the pipeline does. If you have a list of potential buyers, you have information about the market. You have data to tell you a sale is coming, even if it isn't the one you expected. Success is in the percentages, not in winning every time."

I nodded as I watched the exchange between the sales experts. "What happens if your price is *never* too high?" Abe asked, allowing either of us to answer.

Adam waited. I think he knew the answer but wanted to see if I did. I asked, "Do you mean if you get every sale without a price objection?"

"That's exactly what I mean." Abe said with excitement.

I thought about it and concluded accurately, "It probably means you're pricing too low." As I often did with Abe, I answered correctly, but with a tone that suggested it was more of a question.

Adam chimed in. "Yes. If every buyer says your price is right, then it means you're too low. We're supposed to lose some sales. It's the nature of the process. It means you probably should raise your prices."

I looked at Adam and said, "How do you know how much to raise your prices?"

He paused and waited. Abe watched to see where our conversation would go until Adam finally said, "Raise them as much as the market will bear."

As Adam uttered the words, Abe raised a finger to let us know an interjection was coming. He started to speak and then stopped. It was another one of his moments when he analyzed selling intensely. We waited until he said, "I've actually said that before…to both of you. I'm suddenly not sure it's entirely correct. Most people will tell you to charge whatever the market will bear. I also would have said that moments ago and, in fact, I believe it to be true for the small volume accounts and for consumer goods.

"As I think more about our larger clients, there is more to consider. The factors of doing business become more complex. Each buyer has a unique business model, volume differentiation, varying expectations, purchasing practices, and more. Perhaps the most important factor is the long-term dollar-volume consistency you can count on year in and year out. You select the buyers who are a best fit for your personal business model.

"You are your own market. It's what you prove your worth, not the market at large. The best lawyers, doctors, consultants, and even hair stylists charge fees based upon their reputations, not the market. Their reputations are measured by how much people demand their time. As business grows, they up their fees. There are limits to their time and it is no different for you or top sales performers. You increase the value of your time by working efficiently with the choice buyers in the market and by elevating your margins. Getting your price is a matter of self-esteem.

"You build it and, as you evolve, you become more confident pricing new clients at higher margins. It's not a 'test' of the market. Your worth is proven by the unspoken testimonials of other buyers. They vote with their loyalty to you at higher margins. You create power as you mature in your career and build a base of desirable clients while replacing undesirable ones, no different than other professionals who escalate their fees as they grow."

Adam and I were quiet. Abe proved that the concept of self-worth is more important than the market. It's not a price for goods; *it's the price for goods and services rendered*. "The important lesson to learn," Abe said to conclude his train of thought, "is that the more prospects and information you have about opportunities in the market, the more confidence you build in holding your price. Agreed?"

"Q.E.D." I said. Adam looked at me quizzically and I explained what Q.E.D. stood for. He chuckled before asking if that was an 'Abe thing' or a 'Noah thing.' I confessed, "I learned it from Abe, but it's old. It's Latin. So now it's my thing." Adam smiled. Abe beamed.

Abe pointed out that it's not enough to keep prospecting information in your head. "It requires way more information than you can retain in your memory. You need to track your prospecting activity. You need the *performance metrics*. There are a lot of them, but your list of prospects and their values is the key."

It makes sense. More information about sales leads equals more evidence. More evidence of abundance builds negotiation confidence. That's how you build the confidence to beat the price objection before it even occurs. That's how you clean up dirty water in the middle of the river. Maximize *and track* your alternative options.

10

Stop Bidding and Start Proposing

"Stop bidding and start proposing," Abe said. "That's today's lesson."

I looked at him and asked, "Aren't they the same thing?"

"Not even close," he said in a way that was not the least bit cold, but instead delivered as objective coaching guidance. "A bid is a subset of the proposal. The bid includes the products you'll deliver at a price. Usually, it defines payment terms and perhaps has some other legal mumbo jumbo.

"A proposal is different. It connects you to the buyer by demonstrating your understanding of their situation. It enables you to illustrate why your offer is unique. Five bids from five different suppliers will all look the same. A proposal stands out to prove that you are truly different than your competition. Remember how we walked Jessica Sanders through the process by considering Theodore, the dog, in her proposal?"

I nodded while remembering it was purely Abe's sales guidance but nevertheless felt grateful he included me as a contributor to the dialogue. He continued, "It also sets parameters for the relationship. It defines a future contract by outlining your commitment and, at the same time, your expectations of the buyer. Most importantly, it gives the buyer confidence to know you truly do bring better service and value than your competition. It defines your value promise."

"What's a value promise?" I asked.

"Most people say they have a value proposition. I don't care for that term because it only *proposes* to bring value. I like to promise. The buyer should know, *before* you do business, what to expect when you *do* do business."

Abe sat with me in the bullpen. His clean notepad was the only item on the conference table when he started asking me questions.

"What do you really know about Mahogany Builders and John Henderson?" he asked.

It took me only an instant to proudly say, "They are having problems with their existing supplier. It's pretty clear from John's comments and the things I learned from Jimmy. They use a higher-grade product than other builders and they like their homeowners to be involved when choosing windows. So that alone is pretty good information to work with, right?"

Abe scribbled notes while listening to me. After I shared my thoughts, he asked, "What problems are they having with their supplier?"

"Delays. Incomplete orders," I said with finality.

Abe wrote those two words down and asked, "What does that do to Mahogany Builders?"

"It slows them down," I said, wondering why we would belabor an obvious point. Abe waited and I added, "So it costs them money."

"Good," Abe said. "How?"

I answered, again without taking much time to consider his questions. "Time is money. Each delay costs him time, which is money." I was speaking in the clichés salespeople use because they don't realize what it is they don't know until I finally asked Abe, "Right?"

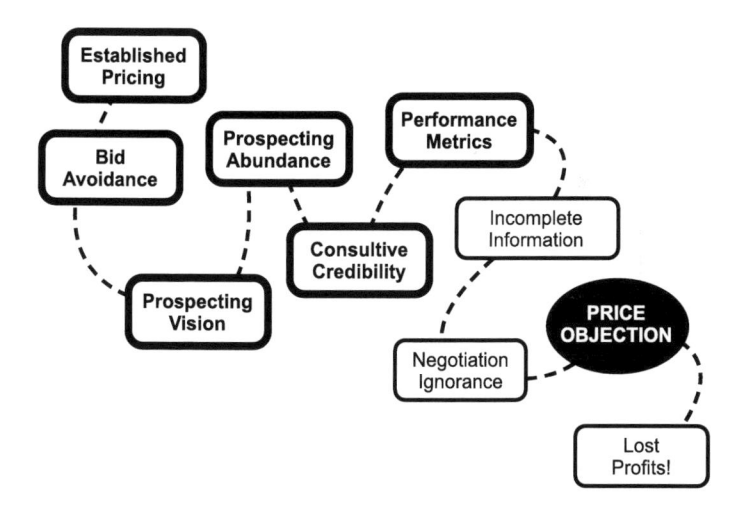

[Diagram showing connections between: Established Pricing, Bid Avoidance, Prospecting Abundance, Performance Metrics, Consultive Credibility, Incomplete Information, Prospecting Vision, Negotiation Ignorance, PRICE OBJECTION, Lost Profits!]

"It's absolutely right, but not complete," Abe said before pointing to the board where his drawing read *incomplete information*. "If you give John a price under the current circumstances, what is it that will set you apart from your competitors?"

"You mean *our* competitors?" I asked, trying to be clever by reminding him we work for the same company.

Abe said, "Nope. I mean *your* competitors. Most salespeople fail to realize that selling is a one-on-one competition. Two salespeople at different companies are competing. One is trying to bring business in for his customer, which is his employer, while you are trying to bring business in for yours.

"If you switched the salespeople to opposite companies, I believe the same salesperson would win. As much as I hate to admit it, our products are usually pretty similar. It is the salesperson who makes the difference by bringing advantages to the buyer.

"So, my question stands. If you provide a price today to Mahogany Builders, what will differentiate you?"

I thought I should say we bring the best value but could hardly define it. Nevertheless, I told Abe, "I'll tell John that I can't guarantee the lowest price, but I can give him the best service."

Abe smiled and asked me which auto dealer in our market has the most cars and will not be undersold?"

I chuckled and understood Abe's point immediately. "Right," I said with a smile. "They *all* promise that. If I promised better service, I'm no different than the rest, right?"

Abe nodded. Then he added, "I hear salespeople use lots of cliché phrases. They say things like you just said or 'You can choose between product, service, or price. You can get two out of three, but you can't get them all.' Some pridefully assert 'I can't promise I'll be the cheapest…' and leave their sentence hanging without justifying *why* they won't be.

"These are trite platitudes," Abe concluded, "crutches to support salespeople who aren't digging deeply enough to define ways they bring tangible and measurable profits to their buyers. Price matters. But there is more. So how will you differentiate yourself from your competitor?"

Abe was putting me to the test, and I was cornered. In that moment, most salespeople get defensive. In my case, I knew Abe was pushing me. He expected me to dig deeply to learn an important concept. If sales braggarts were forced, as I was in that moment, to really think about the advantages they personally bring to the table, they would struggle.

Abe could see my difficulty and said, "A moment ago you said, 'time is money.' You're exactly right. Now I want you to consider *how* time costs money. Can you tangibly quantify how much money is lost by a late delivery?"

I thought for a moment and realized operational costs were a theory to me, not something I could calculate with accuracy. Abe waited patiently until asking me how John Henderson financed his homes. I thought for a moment and concluded he probably went to a bank. "Good!" Abe said. "Now we're onto something. What interest do you suppose the bank charges?"

I didn't know. Abe agreed he didn't either, but made a guess and said, "Let's say it's 5%. So, if John borrows a few hundred thousand dollars of materials and starts racking up debt before he sells a house, how much interest is in each $100,000?"

The math was easy. "$5,000."

"Perfect," Abe said. "If you calculate the interest on a $1,000,000 construction loan, it's $50,000 per year. That's a large investment and means delays are well over $100 per day!

Maybe he has penalties if he doesn't finish the job on time. The truth is we don't know all the facts yet, correct?"

I nodded. Part of me was unsure how this related to a product quote, but I was starting to recognize how much I didn't understand, which was good. Abe says the moment you realize how much you don't know is when you are really starting to become an expert. He asked me what other costs occurred when a product order was delayed. I thought about it and said, "Production shuts down."

Abe nodded and wrote a couple more words on the paper. "Besides the $100 per day, how does this create more costs?" he asked.

I reflected on the question and said, "I guess the first thing is that all the other trades are delayed. It probably means that Jimmy has to reschedule everyone else on the production line." After further envisioning the day-to-day activity at the jobsite, I added, "I am sure they get nervous about damage from the weather, possible theft of other materials already delivered to the jobsite, and…I expect Jimmy doesn't sleep to well at night wondering how he'll explain delays to John."

Abe smiled and said, "Now you're getting it. Do you think John loses any sleep? Who does he have to explain to?"

"His customer," I said correctly.

"Let's get back to a previous question and figure out the most obvious tangible cost of production delays. If the delivery is an hour late, how much does that cost John Henderson?"

"Do you mean besides financing costs and scheduling headaches?"

"That's exactly what I mean," Abe said. "We were at a job site with five laborers if we include Jimmy. If they are stalled for an hour, that is the hourly rate per person times 5. I would guess it costs John well over $50 per laborer on the job if you include salaries, benefits, insurance, and cost of equipment on the job. That's $250 per hour."

I admitted, "I haven't put myself in the buyer's shoes. I haven't thought enough about their business. I need to do that more."

"That's it," said Abe. "You are listening, but not hearing from their perspective. You were listening to sell, not to help. You heard about all the opportunities being presented to you as someone making a sale but failed to connect to the buyer's big picture challenges. John doesn't buy windows or build houses for a living. He sells them. Do you understand?"

I nodded. "Good," Abe said. "If you sell engine blocks to a car manufacturer, they don't buy on features and benefits alone. In fact, they dictate the product specifications to eliminate any differentiation between products. The differentiation between suppliers is based purely on delivery capabilities. If engine blocks are late, the entire system shuts down. Therefore, the manufacturer needs a dependable supplier that keeps the assembly line moving. A good salesperson understands their product might only be one part of a larger production machine. They understand how their product fits into the schedule, yes?"

If the car manufacturer can save a few dollars per engine block, but at the cost of undependable delivery, does the manufacturer actually save money?

"No. Obviously it runs up the cost of production," I conceded.

"Good! The total cost of a product is greater and far more

important than the price. The price is how much the buyer pays for materials. The total cost is the price *plus* factors that enable the buyer to profit. What do you think? Is price the biggest consideration or is it total cost?"

I smiled and said, "It's total cost. But will the buyer actually take the time to factor all that in?"

Abe wisely said, "Not necessarily. A lot will, but some won't. Many buyers will instinctively recognize the lower total cost but negotiate anyway figuring that the salesperson hasn't figured it out. It's not the buyer's job to let you know the financial benefits you bring to the table. You have to figure it out with them and for them.

"There is more," Abe said without stopping. "Cost is the price, installation costs, time value of money and more. On the other side of the ledger, a good product might enable the buyer to elevate pricing.

"Think about it, "Abe said. "People pay more for brand named potato chips, appliances, and cars for no other reason than perceived value. In the same way, some brand names are popular enough to warrant a higher market price to the house buyer by creating more perceived value in the home. We have one of those brands."

I nodded. Abe proved to me that profitability is infinitely more important than a price. A higher price is worth it if it justifies a higher resale price. It is also worth the investment when it reduces production costs. Most importantly, the salesperson must be able to measure the value for the buyer. Elevated profit for the buyer is not a concept; it's a number.

"Is price the biggest consideration for John at this moment?"

I said, "I think it matters a lot, yes."

Abe asked, "Are you the only window supplier competing for the next house?"

I said, "Probably not, but I don't know who else they might be. John *did* send the owner of his next house to our showroom and they really liked the product."

Abe asked, "Has John directed the owner to another showroom?"

I admitted I didn't know.

"Has John told other salespeople to go meet Jimmy at the jobsite?"

Again, I didn't know.

"Have other salespeople given Jimmy the level of details you have?"

I shrugged because, again, I didn't know. I told Abe how hard I worked to give Jimmy the correct sizing and met with his team in case any of them needed to reach me.

"Interesting," Abe said with a strange and knowing smile. I figured the interesting thing was my lack of understanding. He continued. "Let me ask you another question. Why is John considering a change of window suppliers?"

I thought about it and let the question sink in. I recalled the numerous meetings I had with John and the couple of interactions with Jimmy. I thought about all the information they shared and the things I observed.

I said, "Keeping his customer happy is job #1. His current supplier is jeopardizing that, which can cost him money and his reputation. Also, Jimmy told me how he keeps the jobsite clean at the end of every day in case the owner comes by. Last week he reminded me I needed to be perfectly accurate on the window sizes, so he doesn't have to go back and fix mistakes.

BEAT THE PRICE OBJECTION

John has told me that he ensures happy customers so he can get more referrals and build his reputation. He once told me, 'I golf with my customers and see them every day. I can't afford a slip up.'"

Abe scribbled a few more notes and then looked up at me with gleaming eyes. "You heard a lot. Great comments! These are very good observations. So how do you think you can help these gentlemen with their situation?"

He smiled and let me ponder the question. In past coaching sessions, Abe focused a lot on prospecting and listening skills. Now he was showing me how to use those listening skills to craft a proposal that outclasses my competition and influences a positive buying decision.

"I'm going to make doing business with me the easiest thing they have ever done," I said proudly. I meant it.

"That's a great answer! How?"

"I'm going to make sure their orders are detailed properly and put into the system on time. I know, on a few occasions they had to redo past work, which drove up labor and material costs. They also told me they get frustrated when they can't get hold of their salesperson. Therefore, I'm going make sure all their people have my cell phone, not just John and Jimmy. Anyone can call me, and I'll help them get their house built right."

After jotting down his final notes, Abe ripped off the sheet from his notepad and started a clean new one. The paper on which he had been writing was a jumble of ideas scattered all over the page. It was completely disorganized. He looked at me and said, "That was the brainstorming. I expect you to do this on your own at some point. This is how you craft a proposal. You first brainstorm for ideas and then organize them to include with your price offer."

He started to look at his papers to write, but I interrupted him. "What do you mean by price offer? Did you mean bid?"

He looked up and said, "Nope. A bid is something you do at an auction. Remember our conversation about the 'blind reverse auction?' We're not delivering an asking price. We're defining how we produce the lowest total cost and/or the greatest profit for them. It's a telling price."

Abe quietly started writing more on a clean piece of paper. He looked back and forth between his "brainstorming" sheet and the one on which we outlined a proposal. On his clean sheet of paper, Abe wrote *Key Issues* just as he had in Jessica's office the day he started his "dirty water" thesis. He then listed bullet points before writing a new section header, *The Mahogany Builders Window Game Plan*. Under that he added more bullet points. He added a couple sections until his thoughts were complete.

Abe turned the document toward me and asked me what I thought about it. Truthfully, I thought it was weird. I had never seen anything like it. As I read it more closely, I considered what John might think if *he* read it. The first things Abe wrote were about John and his business.

I read Abe's words carefully while he waited patiently. I looked up and said, "This is kind of cool, but I don't remember anyone saying they wanted to 'wow' their customer with a superior experience."

"That's okay," Abe said. "Let me ask you what you think of someone who wants to wow their customer with a superior experience?"

I laughed and said it's a great idea. Abe said, "Then make it yours. If they say they never said it, then you say, 'Oh. Well, then I guess I didn't hear correctly, because it sure seems like that's what you do. You clean the job site. You ensure elated customers. It feels like you really 'wow' them.'"

"It would at least be a great compliment," I said.

Abe smiled. "It would be at least that. Maybe they'd hear it and consider that you bring new ideas to the table. Maybe it would be a term they start using in their company language or marketing promotion. It is the beginning of you differentiating yourself from the competition, because you're talking about your customer's business instead of your own products."

Proposal for Mahogany Builders

Key Issues
- Your goal is to "wow" your customers with a superior experience.
- You socialize and network with your clients.
- Your brand and reputation are built on elated customers.
- Window deliveries are delaying your production.
- It is important that your clients approve product selections.
- You require suppliers that support your sales and production.

The Mahogany Builders Window Game Plan
- I will take responsibility to get order details right.
- I will coordinate delivery schedules with Jimmy and my team.
- We will store and deliver windows screens until construction is complete.
- Everyone on your team will have access to call me.
- Your team's cooperation with me is critical to success.
- We will be the easiest company you do business with.

Product List and Specifications (Attached)

Price and Payment Terms (Attached)

Signed: Noah Foster

Stop Bidding and Start Proposing

Abe added, "The first time we met John, he talked about his word-of-mouth approach to sales. He said he gets a lot of his sales leads from successful business professionals at his golf club and networking referrals. What do you think John will feel when he reads your proposal?" Abe asked.

After a moment of thought I said, "He'll know I've got his back. I've got him covered."

"How will you have him covered?" Abe asked.

At first, I couldn't think of my answer and then Abe cleared his throat comically to get my attention before putting his finger squarely on the paper where it read "The Mahogany Builders Window Game Plan." The bullet points were all the things I said I could do to help. Seeing them in black and white reminded me of the responsibilities I promised to fulfill. I grinned at Abe and said, "That's how I'll have him covered."

"Perfect," said Abe with an approving smile. "It's important to write them down because he'll know what you do to earn your price. It also serves to remind you of your self-worth in the heat of negotiation battle. You're putting your reputation on the line. If you're not going to commit to these things, then don't write them in your proposal. If you are, then you've taken a step to clean up the dirty water at the mouth of the river."

I told Abe I would commit to each one of them. He smiled and said he believed me.

He went to his whiteboard where he had been constructing all his thoughts leading up to the dirty water at the mouth of the river. He erased *incomplete information* and wrote the words **Comprehensive Proposal**. He sat back down and said, "A detailed proposal doesn't guarantee you'll get the business. It won't even guarantee the buyer will accept your price without negotiation. But hopefully you agree, Noah, it is a lot better than just dropping off a product list and a price."

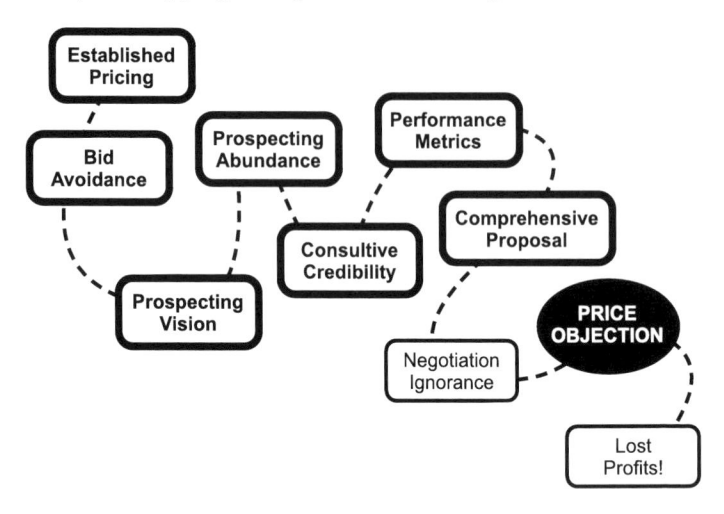

```
Established Pricing
Bid Avoidance
Prospecting Abundance
Performance Metrics
Consultive Credibility
Comprehensive Proposal
Prospecting Vision
Negotiation Ignorance
PRICE OBJECTION
Lost Profits!
```

"I do agree," I said. "The proposal reminds me I need to listen better, um…upstream I guess we could say. If you haven't listened you can't really write a proposal this good."

I remembered how I felt when I was the paying customer. When my wife and I bought a new washer and dryer, one salesperson pushed us to buy the affordable brand. He presumed we were on a limited budget because we were young and starting out in life. The salesperson we actually purchased from asked us about our available space, budget, and lifestyle. She sold us the more expensive model because we were shown it was a better long-term investment.

I remembered when I bought a car; one salesperson tried to sell me a payment plan while the one I eventually bought from asked about my job and how I would use the vehicle. She reminded me that the samples in my trunk and extensive mileage would wear on the engine. She ultimately helped me choose the most suitable one for my job, which happened to be a little more expensive than the one from the salesperson at the other dealership.

In both cases, the washer-dryer and the car purchase, salespeople were representing the identical products of their competitors; it proved Abe's point that selling is not company versus company. It's one-on-one, person-to-person competition.

I didn't regret spending more money with either salesperson and realized the added information about using the products and how they fit into my lifestyle was essential in making the right decision. I looked down at the paper with Abe's handwriting and asked, "Why did you put in those bullet points about his team working with me and the need for cooperation? That kind of puts pressure on them, doesn't it?"

Abe said, "Only if they think it's pressure. You want cooperative clients, don't you?"

I nodded and Abe said, "Then let them know that. It's not for your benefit. It's for theirs!"

He added, "It's only fair. The one thing you can never know about a customer before the relationship begins is how cooperative they will be. Therefore, you remind them up front that your ability to do the job well will only happen if you are given the right information on time. Make sense?"

I nodded.

Abe told me I should put all the other information – i.e.: the product list, product specifications, price, and payment terms – for the first order on a separate sheet and include them with "Key Issues" and the "Mahogany Builders Window

Game Plan." He told me I should print the information on company letterhead, hand deliver the proposal, and review it with John. I did.

All the preparation and work that went into the proposal is in the forefront of my consciousness as John lets it rest on his desk while awaiting my answer to his challenge. A second earlier he said, "Your price is too high. You'll have to come down a bit."

My instinct is to say, *"Let me see what I can do."* I know it is not the answer, but it is an easy one. Abe calls this phrase the "hero's lament." They are the words unprepared salespeople use. He says it's a way to deflect responsibility and shift the negotiation onus to the management level. It allows salespeople to be heroes to customers by negotiating on their behalf instead of with them. "It's not the best solution," Abe says.

As I am hearing John's words, Abe's last negotiation lesson pings in my brain. There is a right way to negotiate. It is the way Abe taught me on the same day he taught to stop bidding and start proposing.

I told Abe that day when he helped craft my proposal, "I agree the proposal establishes the value of my price. But what if John still wants to negotiate. Certainly, there are times to negotiate, yes?"

Abe leaned back and conceded the point, "Of course!"

"But I still don't know how to negotiate when I might have to," I told him.

Abe smiled and said, "You already have the answer, and you don't even know."

11

The Heat of Battle is Too Late

"If I already know, then I'm not sure what it is I know."

Abe smiled and asked, "Remember my patented bid avoidance technique? What are the things you must learn about a buyer before pricing?" I scoured my brain and, even though Abe had me take notes a few weeks ago during his "bid avoidance" lesson, I could only think of two items of his technique – service and delivery expectations. I hadn't properly committed his entire list to memory.

"I'm sorry. I should have memorized them," I said to Abe. He waved off my apology and was neither angry nor disappointed. Instead, he made a comment that had more impact.

"It's not about me, Noah. It's about you. You never owe me an apology," he said. "You decide how skilled you want to be. Truthfully, you don't have to agree with me or even use the techniques I share. I'm not asking you *to* believe a word I say. I'm asking *if* you believe an idea. And if so, what you will *do* with it?"

It was a little embarrassing because I did agree with his ideas and thought I had been using his "bid avoidance" tactic properly. I slowed the process with high-pressure buyers but hadn't accessed the full potential of "bid avoidance" by understanding the details and nuances of the information.

He looked at his notepad and started writing. When he was finished, four items were noted in bullet points under the caption *Negotiation 101 – Get to Give*. "*Volume* and *cross-selling*," Abe said. "Those are two of the other things you should know before pricing. *Service, delivery, volume,* and *additional products the buyer might add to the sale*. Does the list look familiar?" he asked while turning his paper toward me. The items on his "bid avoidance" technique were, interestingly enough, the exact same items to seek in a price negotiation.

**NEGOTIATION 101 –
"Get to Give"
Trade Concessions**

- Delivery
- Service
- Volume
- Other products you can add
- How the buyer makes money and succeeds

"Yes," I said, understanding fully. "If a buyer wants a better price, I should ask for a delivery or service concession…or for a commitment for more volume…or the opportunity to sell additional products…or help them make money."

He took back the notepad and wrote more. I watched and waited without bothering to tell Abe I wouldn't forget the items on his "bid avoidance" list again. There was no value in doing so because he valued actions more than promises. He recognized good performance.

"Well done is better than well said," Abe would say, citing the wisdom of Ben Franklin. I would make it my business to continue improving my performance and let my actions speak louder than my words.

"The technique you use is 'Get to Give.' It is a fundamental skill for salespeople," Abe explained. "Call it 'Sales Negotiation Skills 101.' It's the first negotiation lesson any salesperson must absorb. If you are asked to give something, you should get something in return. The trick is knowing what to get before negotiations start. You will never succeed in the heat of battle until you prepare prior to it."

Our discussion made me realize that I deal with buyers who probably take classes and learn during "*Buyers* Negotiation Skills 101" to always test the waters to see how a salesperson will react. They deal with so many salespeople who cave quickly under pressure, like I'm on the verge of doing with John, that it becomes foolish in their minds not to ask.

Abe asked, "What are some delivery or service concessions you might request to justify the lower price?"

I paused and couldn't think of any, to which Abe said, "The heat of battle is too late. Preparation is the difference between success and failure. If you think it's hard now, wait until you're in the emotional throes of a negotiation. That's why I call it negotiation ignorance. It's not a matter of intelligence; it's preparation."

Abe wrote a list of concessions to seek in response to a negotiation for a lower price. After he jotted his notes, he looked up and said, "Now here is the important thing. You must get your concession *before* you agree to a lower price. If you say, 'I think I can do a little better, but would you be willing to make a sacrifice to justify it?' the buyer will hear that you have already agreed to a lower price and resist offering any concession in return. If you instead make your offer conditional on a trade, you'll set yourself up for a better outcome. You ask, 'IF I could get a better price for you, and I'll need to check on that, would you be willing to do X?'

Abe continued, "X, in this case, could be one of the concessions listed here, or numerous others." He turned the sheet of paper to me. It included an essential negotiation reminder, specifically to gain a concession before agreeing to the price.

I looked down at the paper where it listed *service, delivery, volume,* and *other products,* and *how the buyer makes money or succeeds*. I smiled and looked up. "I ask for a service or delivery concession. Or I ask for more volume. Or more products."

Abe smiled. "Excellent!"

> **NEGOTIATION 101 –**
> **"Get to Give"**
> **Trade Concessions**
>
> - Delivery – e.g. flexible timing; customer pickup.
> - Service – e.g. product lists; pre-payment.
> - Volume – commitment for future business.
> - Other products you can add.
> - How the buyer makes money and succeeds.
>
> IMPORTANT: Get acceptance of the trade before you agree to lower your price.

"Write down these words down and memorize them," Abe said. He watched me take a pen in hand and said, *"I'm not sure I could give you a better price. I have to look into it. Before I do, I have to ask: Would you be willing to give me X…in exchange for a price concession?"* Abe went slowly so I could write it all down. I finished writing the phrase and he stopped talking. I was waiting for the rest. That is when he asked me, "So, what should you seek in exchange for a lower price? What is the X?'"

Before I could answer I told Abe, "The 'If I could, would you..' technique feels kind of like a used car salesman." Like a lot of young salespeople, and probably many veterans, I wasn't comfortable engaging in aggressive negotiation dialogues.

"It's not an ultimatum or demand. It's an offer," Abe said. "If it feels like a tactic for a used car salesman, then so be it. It's a tactic you use for a very specific situation. If you're going to encounter a combative negotiator, you need combative tactics. If this situation arises, you need to be prepared."

124 BEAT THE PRICE OBJECTION

He educated me further by saying, "There are three types of negotiations – collaborative, compromising, and combative. Your goal is to always turn a combative negotiation into a compromise. And remember what we talked about; a concession granted too easily doesn't feel like a victory if the buyer is left wondering whether they left money on the table. You should also trust, as hard as it may be to believe, the aggressive response is what the combative negotiator respects.

"You will encounter collaborative negotiators too. You will discover that the relationships you have with clients evolve from combative or compromising to collaborative. That takes time and proof that you can really do the job well."

I asked, "Can you actually find collaborative buyers who don't make you go through all the hassle of negotiations?"

Abe beamed. "Great question and the answer is…yes! It's part of prospecting. Do you remember when we talked about *prospecting vision*?" Abe asked while pointing to his diagram on the board. I remembered it well. It was the vision to find fair-minded, low-hassle buyers who are very cooperative. He reminded me again of Charley Moore, my customer who has been cooperative from the start. He's loyal, easy to do business with, and never balks at my price. "You said you 'wished you could have a lot more customers like him.'

"See? It all works as a system, like the water in a river," Abe explained. "It's the dirty water you clean upstream before it's too late. Part of beating the price objection is as simple as prospecting for the right buyer. That's why prospecting abundance and measurement matter so much. The more you prospect, the likelier it is you'll find the right buyers and, as importantly, build confidence to walk away from unreasonable negotiations. It all starts with prospecting.

"If you find a cooperative buyer, there is less dirty water downstream in the price negotiation. If you encounter a combative negotiator, you know how to cope. If you avoid bidding blindly and walk away from prospects who won't invest time to hold a preliminary discussion, you save more time to prospect for collaborative buyers. It all ties together.

"A lot of factors go into profit enhancement. Everything we've been talking about comes into play. Your profits are not determined in the final moments of the negotiation. The negotiation is a portion of the profit enrichment process, not the sum total."

I stared at Abe's simple sheet. It seems so obvious, although it hadn't been until he outlined it.

"It astounds me," Abe said, "how many experienced salespeople encounter the price objection and are not prepared. It's hardly a surprising moment. It should be expected." On that day he walked to his whiteboard and replaced *negotiation ignorance* with **Negotiation Planning**. As he was writing, I realized how many times and in different ways buyers had told me my price was too high.

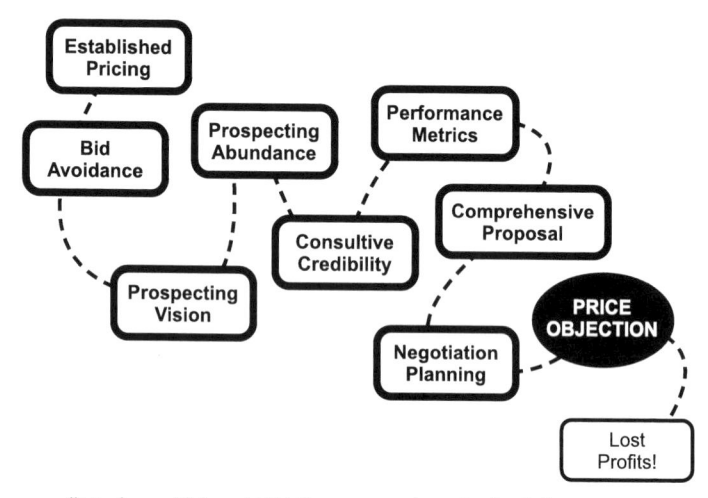

126 BEAT THE PRICE OBJECTION

```
Established
 Pricing
    |
    |         Prospecting      Performance
  Bid         Abundance         Metrics
Avoidance                           \
    \           |                    \
     \          |              Comprehensive
      \         |                Proposal
       \     Consultive
        \   Credibility
         \      |              PRICE
      Prospecting              OBJECTION
        Vision
                    Negotiation
                     Planning
                                    \
                                     Lost
                                    Profits!
```

"You're off by 10%," one said, which I knew was an unreasonable anchor. Dozens more had flatly stated I "came in too high." Others, like John, said, "You'll have to do better." The ways in which our price is said to be too high is infinite yet, until now, I had not prepared adequate countermeasures.

Abe and I discussed potential concessions a bit longer. It felt great to be treated more like an equal than an employee. I came up with my own ideas that Abe endorsed. We agreed that a service concession could be an agreement to shift responsibilities for after-sale service or, even better, payment terms. I suggested we could ask for a buyer to pre-pay for products as an incentive to lower the price one percent or pay cash instead of sticking us for credit card fees. He loved the ideas. He said that a delivery concession could be a bulked shipment or even a customer pickup. Ideas flowed and I was feeling more confident about the moments when I would face a tough negotiation.

The Heat of Battle is Too Late

The negotiation options are now flashing confidently through my mind. I feel like a Marvel comic's superhero dispassionately analyzing the complex situation before him. Inside the helmet screen of my high-tech suit, the red lettering digitizes a menu of concessions I could ask of John to justify his price request. The prevailing thought is to ask for a commitment for more sales volume, but I decline that option because I know he'll give me the business anyway if I do a good job. No need to set a precedent for a lower price based on that consideration.

I'm resistant to reduce my personal commitment to managing project details because it would result later in John's dissatisfaction. Negotiating payment terms doesn't seem like an option and I can't think of a product I can add to the package because, unlike some of my competitors, I only sell windows. The multitude of issues learned over months is overwhelming me as I flash back.

"Remember what we said about the psychology of a quick concession granted in the heat of negotiation," Abe said. "If you just willy-nilly lower your price, the buyer will eventually wonder if they got your *best* price. You might leave them wondering if they should have gotten 2 percent instead of 1… or 3 percent instead of 2. They won't even know it immediately, but it is a potential psychological outcome.

"So…if you are going to lower your price, you need to get something in return. It is the way you save your reputation and make your buyer feel good about the transaction." Abe continued, "The 'get to give' strategy allows you to save face by assuring the buyer you were not trying to take advantage of them. Instead, you're asking for a small, low-cost concession from the buyer to justify a reasonable exchange in value.

"There is one more option," Abe said. "It's the 'Give to Hold' negotiation strategy."

At this point, I just laughed and thought, *of course Abe has another strategy.* "What is it?" I asked, still chuckling.

"Look at that last item I said you should understand before you bid," Abe said, pointing to his paper on the list of concessions. The last one didn't have anything to do with the transactional factors of deliveries, service, volume, or products. It was about the buyer's business.

I looked at the paper. "*How the buyer makes money…*" I said as my voice trailed off to think about the relationship between this and a price negotiation.

"Instead of lowering your price," Abe said, "give something to hold it. We'll call it the 'Give to Hold' strategy. You offer the buyer something of low-cost to you and high value to them. For instance, provide an extra delivery to help the buyer manage the production schedule and reduce waste on the job. Perhaps offer training services to your customer's employees. Maybe you could take on extra responsibility. We could ship the product in parts to reduce damage. These are benefits that come at a slight cost to you and the company while producing high monetary value for the buyer."

Abe reminded me, "In business-to-business selling, buyers don't just buy materials. They use them to build their products or often re-sell the goods you sell. If you have properly understood *how* they make money, the 'Give to Hold' strategy offers actions that *help* them make money. You can provide marketing ideas, scheduling convenience, added personal services and more such as a sales lead of an interested prospect for your customer. There are lots of ways you can help your customers make more money from your products and services.

"You matter. Your value and talent are unique. The one thing your buyer can't get from anyone else in the world is *you*. Figure out what you can give, or *already* are giving to justifying your telling price."

The "Give to Hold" options are not coming to me quickly. I already feel like I've given John a lot. My proposal outlined abundant ways in which I would help him succeed, and in fact, I have already provided many ways in which John's team will benefit. I'm prepared to prove my worth. My offer is a personal promise that I will prove not in words, but in actions. It might only be eight pages stapled at the corner, but it hits me now how valuable that proposal is sitting on his desk.

Abe said getting your telling price is a matter of self-esteem and I heard it before I understood it. Now I get it. I have met with John several times to prepare for a successful business relationship and explained it all in my proposal. If I do a good job on his next house, I've *earned* more work. I shouldn't have to lower my price to make that conditional. The value of my personal service will make him more successful financially. He'll deliver a better experience to *his* customers.

The flashing lights and words churn up, down, and across my superhero screen. I wonder if John is seeing a flicker in my eyes as the options roll past. In the midst of agitation, fear, and hope, a moment of epiphany and…Eureka! Power and confidence replace all emotions!

12

Career Security

I'm driving back to the office. The words "Price Objection" are imprinted on my brain. Abe's white board provides a series of insights for each step of the sales journey. He had explained why suggested prices and starting points erode profits. He showed me how salespeople advocate too strongly for their buyers. He demonstrated how important it is to proactively look for profitable customers and the importance of creating an abundance of prospects, specifically the ideal types.

The only difference between sales leadership and mediocrity is the preparation that takes place long before the price objection rears its ugly head. In a perfect world, people would buy at your price without negotiating at all. We live far from a perfect world. There is litter, dust, dirt, emotions, news feeds, personalities, moods, fears, hopes, anxiety, greed,

132 BEAT THE PRICE OBJECTION

competition, and a thousand other factors affecting buying decisions. Sales leadership means preparing for the many situations you will encounter, including the price objection.

The dirty water cannot be cleaned up at the mouth of the river. The pollutants upstream add up. It probably surprises some salespeople to think that their negotiation confidence depends on a lot of factors that have nothing to do with the buyer in front of them. They think it happens only in the moment.

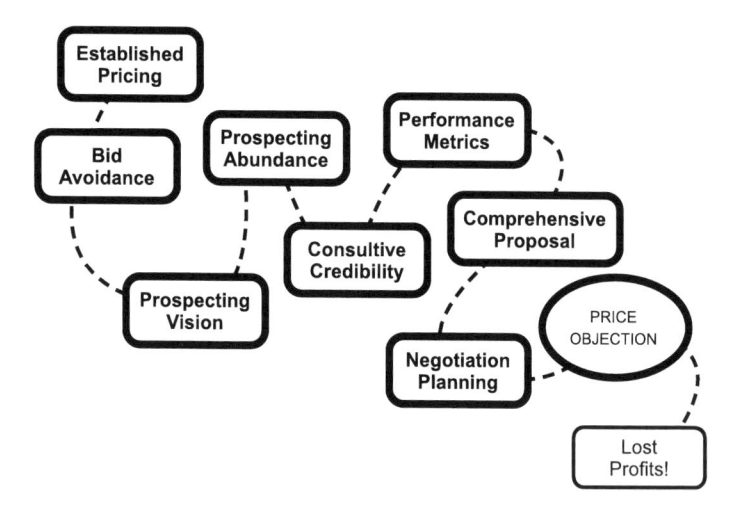

```
Established Pricing
Bid Avoidance
Prospecting Abundance
Performance Metrics
Consultive Credibility
Comprehensive Proposal
Prospecting Vision
Negotiation Planning
PRICE OBJECTION
Lost Profits!
```

I learned that moving too fast and bidding is a sure-fire way to become a price-oriented salesperson. Abe once said that the quick price delivery is like having a drive through window at a fast-food restaurant. Anyone can bid a price, but a true salesperson demonstrates value greater than the price. The "bid avoidance" technique is the first step he taught me to slow things down. It illustrated the ways in which I can establish immediate credibility.

I learned that my role is to run my own business. My customer is my employer, but so is my buyer. I am the middleman who needs to help everyone profit. Prospecting measurement tactics have given me confidence to envision future sales. Instead of just bidding randomly, I am taking time with clients to understand them. I listen carefully and make sure I can really help them. I help my clients succeed at a fair price while ensuring my employer is profitable.

One day I called Abe and told him we were probably not a fit for a difficult prospect. He said my decision symbolized progress as a salesperson. He told me he was proud for me. I liked the way he said he was proud *for* me and not *of* me. There is a difference. He was saying that it wasn't about his approval of me, but instead my approval of myself. Most managers wouldn't allow a salesperson to walk away from a bad sales situation, let alone compliment them for it. Abe encourages it.

He had erased the words *price objection* on his whiteboard during a Monday morning sales meeting with the team. After he erased them, he darkened the border of the box and wrote, as he had for all the other "solutions" to the price objection puzzle, the exact same words. PRICE OBJECTION. This time, the words didn't have nearly the same power as before.

Abe said, "Starting points instead of prices, instant quotes, fear of lost income, a commodity mindset, unreasonable management pressure, incomplete information, and negotiation ignorance. They are pollutants upstream. These are the enemies of profit. You deserve your asking price...*if* you put in the work to help your customers succeed.

"The price objection is out of your control," he added. "It's going to happen. The difference between success and failure

134 BEAT THE PRICE OBJECTION

occurs long before the moment of this predictable obstacle."

The proposal I delivered to John Henderson was proof to myself that I had evolved as a salesperson. I was equipped with numerous negotiation options when he told me my price was too high.

"You might not always get your telling price," Abe conceded. "But you should act and believe as though you are deserving. Our customers can buy products from a lot of companies and people. The one thing they can't buy from anyone is you. You are a one-of-a-kind offer."

My windows are open while U2's *Still Haven't Found What I'm Looking For* is blaring on my sound system. It's the 40th anniversary edition with the New Voices of Freedom Choir as backup. Today I have found exactly what I was looking for, but the music inspires nonetheless. It's one of my go-to happy songs.

My phone rings. It's Abe. I hit the button on my steering wheel and the music is replaced by his voice.

"How did it go?" the wise man is asking me without saying hello. He doesn't even wait for me to call him. Abe always says that a true leader is supportive and helps other people succeed. He had previously told me he wanted to celebrate a sale if it happened and counsel me if it didn't.

I'm replaying the entire story with excitement I can barely contain.

"I delivered my proposal to John, and he turned directly to the last page, exactly as you predicted," I am telling Abe. "He paused and then told me my price was higher than expected.

He said I would have to 'come down a bit.' Everything you've been teaching me went through my brain in a split second until I asked him, 'Did you read the proposal? Did you see all the things I will be doing for you?' Obviously, he hadn't because I was right there and could see.

"I asked if we could at least review it all before we started dickering on price and he realized, I think, that he was being pretty aggressive. We discussed the 'key issues' section you helped me write for the proposal. John smiled and said, 'I admit that no other salesperson has taken the time to understand my business like you.'

"Can you believe it?" I am asking Abe. Silly question. Of course, Abe believes it because he taught it to me, and he is excited about my enthusiasm. He is not pressuring me to finish my story. He's allowing me my moment of glory.

"So," I continue, excited while driving toward a next appointment, "we went through all the details including the game plan of placing the first order. I explained that I'll walk it into Angela in purchasing and double-check the details with her after the order is placed. I assured him that I'm taking personal responsibility for the product getting there on time and in full."

At my company, we talk a lot about getting orders to the customer "on time and in full." Many people assume the job of fulfillment rests with the operations team. Our sales team knows the whole success of an order starts when it is placed. As I think about it, it's another form of dirty water upstream. A production team can't deliver on time unless everything happens correctly early in the process, including order placement.

I have this thought in mind when I explain to Abe what I said next. "'One of two things is going to happen *for* or *to* Mahogany Builders in about six weeks…and it's your call,' I told John. 'One option is to place the order now, hopefully with me, but you have to get your order in soon. If you order with me, the product can be manufactured, delivered to our facility, and staged waiting *for* you the day you need it. Option two is to postpone your order and discover the day you need the windows, they are not available. On that day, the thing that happens *to* you is your production will be shut down. It'll be a fire drill.' Then I told him…

"'You'll call your salesperson and apply pressure to expedite a single order from a multi-million-dollar manufacturing organization located 800 miles away. You'll get lip service and promises to 'see what can be done.' Then your order will still be late. Does that sound at all familiar?'" I am assuring Abe that I wasn't saying these things in anger, but merely explaining what I saw in the future. "I asked John which of those two scenarios he wanted."

"John frowned, but it wasn't really a look of displeasure. He managed a knowing smile at the same time. Clearly he doesn't want to be pushed around, but it felt like I had earned his attention and respect. So, I said, 'John, I value this opportunity more than you know. I really want to be your supplier. The thing I do know is this…

"'If I lower my price, my biggest fear is that I'll lose enthusiasm. I'll consider a lower price an excuse to cut corners. I know it's wrong and not fair. But I think that is what happens when salespeople sacrifice too much. They rationalize that it's okay to lower service standards. I don't want that, and you don't want that. If you do business with me, it has to be at this price. I promised you, when we first started talking, that I would give you my best price…and I did.'"

I can feel Abe's pride over the phone. He asks, "So? What did John say?"

"Nothing, at first," I tell Abe. "And you know that old saying that the first person who talks during a price standoff loses? Well, it's not true. I talked first and told John, 'I don't want to lose this sale. Honestly. But, even if you don't do business with me, I've seen where you're at in your project and know that a delay in ordering now will spell trouble later. You need to get your order in, no matter who you choose to do business with.'"

Abe had long told all his sales students that timing is everything when it comes to closing the sale. Most salespeople try to force timing by getting the order when they want it. Business executives commonly push salespeople to magically manufacture sales when business gets slow. "That's not how it works," Abe says. "If you push for sales when you're desperate, mistakes happen. Your negotiation leverage is weakened.

"Closing is incremental. Closing is timing. In consumer sales, the salesperson can try to manufacture timing. In business-to-business relationships, the timing must be based on the moment it's right for the buyer and their larger schedule."

The timing was right for John Henderson. A decision delay would cost him in a variety of ways. I knew he had to place an order with someone soon and sensed I was the choice he wanted to go with. I concluded he was testing the waters, and you can't blame him. As Abe says, "the willingness of salespeople to negotiate becomes ritualized by buyers, because it so often works, and is supported by our own fears when we cave to the pressure." I was able to understand the situation from John Henderson's perspective and sincerely believe he saw the value I would bring to his organization. I felt no fear and instead believed John would make the best decision by working with me.

Abe tells me, "Of course you already knew, or should have, that you had the sale in the bag and didn't need to lower your price."

I didn't understand his comment. I told him it felt like I was in a good spot, but I didn't feel there were any guarantees if I held my price, but at least I'd buy time if he said, "no."

Abe says, "Do you remember when we wrote your proposal outline? Do you remember what you described? I made a comment. I said 'interesting.' You never asked me what was interesting, so I didn't say."

There is silence and I finally asked, "So what was interesting?"

"You already had the sale," Abe says, "at least from my perspective. You had given Jimmy the opening sizes. The production was just beginning, and his interaction with you was a tell. It was a purchasing signal, an expressed commitment. He implicitly had indicated your windows would be installed in their frames. That is why he demanded your detailed accuracy. I felt it would be a big mistake if you conceded any money, and you didn't. Well done!"

"But why didn't you say something?" I ask incredulously. "What if I had given away a pile of money?"

Abe speaks in words that radiate his smile over the phone, "Because you wouldn't have learned the great experience of facing the storm. You wouldn't have discovered on your own that you are worth every penny of your price. If you sacrificed a little, we would have survived financially, and I would have shared my insights at that moment so you could discover the power of holding your price on a future sale. But obviously that isn't necessary because you did it on your own."

If you think my story is like the end of a detective mystery, you'd be right. The signs were all there and maybe you read them and maybe you didn't. Abe did. He is the detective who quietly amassed all the information in interviews and observations of people. As soon as he presents the evidence, I realize he is right. John was talking tough to me, but the signs were there. He probably didn't realize that Jimmy was inadvertently telling me I had the order wrapped up. Abe saw it. I didn't.

"Courage," Abe says.

"Courage?"

"Yep," Abe says. "You found it. It's as important that you got the sale by holding firm as it would have been by catching the buying signals. Sometimes they won't be clear and, truth be told, I just 'thought' it was a done deal. I could have been wrong. The important thing is that you found the courage to hold your price. Mark Twain said, 'Courage is not the absence of fear; it is the mastery of it.'"

Epilogue:
Going Through the Motions

Now that you've read my story, you might say, "Oh sure, Noah. Now that you tell me everything that went into the sale with Mahogany Builders, I'm hardly surprised you made the sale. You had choices because you prospected and found a lot of other high-quality leads. You delivered a proposal that outlined your value. You knew he was dissatisfied with his current supplier. If you have all that going for you, then of course you'd close the deal."

And you'd be right! If you work to clean up the dirty water at the mouth of the river, it's easy. If you consider that your prices should inspire confidence in buyers instead of doubt, it's easier to sell. If you first understand your buyer's challenges and goals, it's easier. If you create alternatives with abundant prospecting, each sale is not an all-or-nothing pinnacle moment of confrontation.

The moment you start to listen everything changes. You're right that it *is* easier if you understand how your clients make money and manage their operational costs. It *is* easier if you can communicate information relevant to the buyer's success. That was the power of the proposal. It started with the buyer's situation, the most important factor in their decision making.

It is easier if you know, before the battle, when to negotiate and, more importantly, how. If John had refused to accept the price, then I could have negotiated if I wanted to, although in his case I wouldn't.

I was convinced my price was fair. I forgot to tell Abe that his words echoed in my head as I stood on the doorstep of that sale. *You will never know the joy, power, and satisfaction of holding your price and winning a sale until you've held your price and lost one.*

Just as Abe said, "It's not a theory; it's a law. If you are always willing to negotiate, you will never know if you will get the sale at your telling price. Think about it. If you only *intend* to hold your price until the buyer finally draws a line the sand and tells you that you *must* lower your price or lose the sale, it's decision time. Will you stick to your intentions or not? If you don't, you never really delivered a telling price in the first place. You delivered an asking price, which is nothing more than a starting point. At some point during your career, you must lose a sale. It's part of the initiation process, a rite of passage."

The thing that you really learn from the price objection exercise is that it takes a lot of work to become a complete salesperson. You saw the fear I felt at the start of this story. It's a natural reaction and, as I noted, a younger and less experienced version of me would have caved. The nervousness faded quickly. By the time John wielded his price objection, I had confidence and a perception of abundance acquired by prospecting, listening, and sharing valuable resources with existing and potential buyers.

You shouldn't be surprised to learn that Jessica's company, the remodeler from the early part of my story and the inspiration for Abe's theory, has become a very loyal client at a profitable sales margin. I have supported her business by doing more than just getting orders correct and on time. I have provided additional sales ideas and profitable leads for her. I have many more stories of ways in which I've contributed to other customers' successes well beyond the products I provide.

Abe told me the pressure from managers will dissipate when I feel confident in knowing how to achieve results by adhering to a controlled process. He promised me that I would get something much greater than job security. "Job security," Abe said, "is the permission someone else gives you to work for them. Career security occurs when you believe you have skills worth marketing to an employer. The employer is no longer giving you permission to work for them, but instead buying the quality service you bring to the table."

You would think that Abe replaced the words *lost profit* with words about increased profits…or margins…or some form of monetary gain. He didn't. During a sales meeting, he completed his drawing and wrote the words **Career Security** to complete his diagram. He said, "You learn to go through the motions."

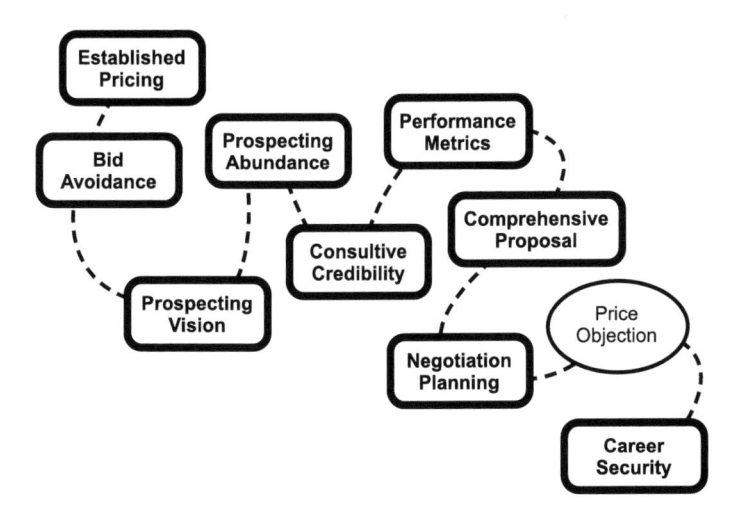

The lesson that resonates most of all is the one Abe delivered when he used those words *go through the motions*. He asked his sales team in the bullpen, during that Monday morning meeting, what it meant to say someone "goes through the motions." We agreed the phrase had negative connotations. It's typically used as an insult about someone who isn't putting their heart into a job.

Abe conceded it was usually meant that way. That's because people going through the motions are performing the wrong tasks or perhaps performing the right ones, but in both cases without energy and heart. In his mind, however, going through the motions means sticking to a plan. It means discovering a process and repeating it until a better method comes along. It means performing the tasks that work. He assured us that it's not "just" going through the motions…if you do it with heart.

He reminded all of us that his "bid avoidance" move is boring and dull after you've done it one hundred times. "But remember," he said. "It's the first time that specific buyer heard it from you. So, go through the motions, but with heart." He reminded us that making dozens of cold calls is boring, but will yield results when done with excellence…and heart.

He reminded us that his proposal format gets boring and tedious until we remember it will be exhilarating for the buyer who sees it for the first time. He told us that memorizing negotiation tactics might be boring, but is essential and invaluable when used comfortably in a pressure moment.

I think about a sale I lost because, instead of asking the potential buyer about her business challenges as Abe taught, I focused on product issues. I didn't get the sale because I hadn't established the right connection by going through the motions of sincerely understanding her business. I think about a sale I lost because I didn't go through the motions of writing a meaningful proposal, but instead e-mailed only the product list and price to a prospective new client. I think about the many times I gave up a small percentage of the price because I didn't go through the motions of learning and employing fundamental negotiation tactics.

The thing I learned from Abe was more than the process of cleaning up the price objection long before it rears its ugly head at the mouth of the river. I learned that the ability to do the process once with excellence gave me the ability to do it over and over again. I learned that success is not a sudden moment in time, nor does it happen overnight. I learned that job security might be something another person bestows upon you. Career security, however, is something much greater. It's knowing you have the ability to go through the motions of success and never have to worry about a job again because you've created a set of career skills.

Success creeps up on you when you're not looking. Success happens when you stick to a game plan. Success is unnoticeable in the moment but reveals itself in large ways over time. Success happens when you keep busy going through the motions…with heart.

About the Author

RICK DAVIS is a sought-after speaker, trainer, sales consultant, and the president of Building Leaders, Inc. This is Rick's fourth book on sales. He is also a world class magazine columnist who has been awarded gold and silver medals from the American Society of Business Publishing Editors.

Rick earned his B.A. in Economics while also studying mathematics, computer science, acting, and other classes that he found interesting, like 19th century Russian literature, while attending the University of Michigan. He resides in Chicago, Illinois where he continues to be a curious student of many subjects, all of which he uses to produce universal messages of philosophy and spirituality, mingled with business, that resonate, he hopes, with his audiences.

He is a loving husband of 25 years to his wife, a triathlete, avid long-distance cyclist, poker player, student of all things, pianist, gourmet cook, handy with a screwdriver, dangerous with a miter saw, way above average looking, kind to old people (because he is becoming one), and the possessor of a wonderful sense of humor. You know this must all be true because he wrote this bio himself!

> For more information on keynotes, training,
> or Building Leaders 24/7 online learning platform,
> visit **www.buildingleaders.com**.